T0126259

The Colonial God
YHWH

Norman Habel
Anne Pattel-Gray

The *De-colonising the Biblical Narrative* series is a new landmark in Biblical hermeneutics. The volumes in this series are designed to employ principles for decolonising the text to explore the colonial dimensions of the text and to retrieve pre-colonial narratives that resonate with the Ancestral Narratives of First Nations Peoples.
Series Editor

Anne Pattel-Gray

Norm Habel

1. *A First Nations De-colonising of Genesis 1–11*, edited by Aunty Anne, Uncle Norm and Australian First Nations, 2022.

2. *A First Nations De-colonising of Genesis 12–25*, 2023.

De-colonising
the Biblical Narrative
Volume 3

The Colonial God
YHWH

**Progressive Revelation
of the Character of YHWH
in the Book of Exodus
Uncle Norm (Norman Habel)
Aunty Anne (Anne Pattel-Gray)**

Adelaide
2023

2023 ©copyright remains with Norman Habel & Anne Pattel-Gray

All rights reserved. Except for any fair dealing permitted under the Copyright Act, no part of this book may be reproduced by any means without prior permission. Inquiries should be made to the publisher.

Front cover image: Based on, Artist unknown. From Bryan AL Cochrane, a corroboree ground prepared for a totemic ceremony in central Australia, 1971.

The Australian Aborigines, London, British Museum, 1973.

ISBN:
Softcover: 978-1-922737-96-0
Hardcover: 978-1-922737-97-7
Epub: 978-1-922737-98-4
PDF: 978-1-922737-99-1

SCAN ME

Published and edited by

Making a lasting impact
An imprint of the ATF Press Publishing Group
owned by ATF (Australia) Ltd.
PO Box 234
Brompton, SA 5007
Australia
ABN 90 116 359 963
www.atfpress.com

Contents

Preface

*This volume (volume three) is dedicated
to those First Nations Australia[1] peoples
who were encouraged by colonists—
especially the early missionaries—
to believe in the
Lord God.*

*Early settlers were unaware
that the term 'Lord'
is not a title for God in the Bible.
It is the name of the colonial God
YHWH.*

*This volume reflects
the decolonising approach developed
by Anne Pattel-Gray, Norman Habel,
and other First Nations Australia,
including Ken Sumner, Denise Champion,
Rose Rigney and Sean Weetra.*

---

1. Preferred term to refer to Indigenous peoples by the developers of the decolonising approach.

PART ONE
Introduction
Colonial Consciousness

When Uncle Norm came home to Australia in 1974, he asked the question: what was God[1] doing in Australia before the Europeans came? He soon began to realise that his question was naïve; He should have been asking: what did we think our God was doing when Europeans invaded the country and tried to colonise both the First Nations Australia peoples and their Land?

In recent times along with Uncle Norm, we have begun to comprehend the effect of what some of our First Nations Australia mentors have designated the 'colonial curse'—a factor that has persisted in various forms since the arrival of the first Europeans. For our mentors, the 'colonial curse' refers to all negative effects of the colonial invasion of Australia: everything from stealing the Land to poisoning waters and massacres of men, women and children.

On reflection, we believe we can now identify four stages in the evolution of our 'colonial consciousness'—my inner personal awareness of what the 'colonial curse' has meant for First Nations Australia.

The first stage commenced in the early 1990s.

Working with the Rainbow Spirit Elders, especially George Rosendale, Uncle Norm began to understand the effects the colonial curse, and the depth of the precolonial spiritual culture of First Nations Australia peoples. The Elders declared that the

---

1. In this text, we use the term 'God' to demonstrate the understanding that Gods known by other names share characteristics of the God that Christians believe is the true God revealed to us in the Christian Scriptures by Jesus. First Nations Australia Christians believe, the God known by various names in their languages, is the Creator Spirit who claims all humans are the children of God.

1

> Creator Spirit is known to Aboriginal Australians by many
> names, including Yiirmbal, Biame, Rainbow Spirit, Paayamu,
> Biral, Wandjina and, in Christian times, Father God.[2]

The name of God in Christian times, according to the Rainbow Spirit
Elders, is Father God, the father of Jesus Christ; it is not the colonial
God YHWH who justified the actions of the colonial invaders.

According to the Rainbow Spirit Elders, the colonial curse caused
the Creator Spirit of the Land to cry in agony because the Land was
being desecrated, dispossessed, and polluted with Aboriginal blood.
According to those Elders, the colonial curse traumatised the Land,
the peoples of the Land—and the Creator Spirit in the Land.

As Uncle Norm listened to, and transcribed, the experiences of
the Rainbow Spirit Elders in the volume entitled *Rainbow Spirit
Theology*,[3] his consciousness of the colonial curse began to affect his
faith, his vision, his worldview and his approach to the Scriptures.
By listening to the painful experiences of his Rainbow Spirit Elder
mentors, he became aware that most of his thinking and reading of
the Bible—until the time of that retreat—had been influenced by the
colonial culture of his local community.

The second stage began in 1999 when we worked with a First
Nations group and wrote a volume to promote reconciliation. The
volume, entitled: *Reconciliation: Searching for Australia's Soul*,[4]
includes an appendix: Healing Rites at Seven Sites. The very first rite
reflects an awareness of the curse of colonisation.

In the ritual, an elder cries,

> We begin our journey in Sydney Cove
> where they hoisted the British flag that day,
> a flag unknown to the host nation,
> waiting at a respectable distance.
>
> They hoisted the flag and stole a Land
> they claimed to discover
> in the name of their King
> and with the blessing of their God.

---

2. Rainbow Spirit Elders, *Rainbow Spirit Theology* (Adelaide: ATF Press, 2007), 31.
3. Rainbow Spirit Elders, *Rainbow Spirit Theology*.
4. Norman Habel, *Reconciliation: Searching for Australia's Soul* (Melbourne: Harper Collins, 1999).

'Forget a treaty,' they said.
'There's no one here to stop us,
no one here to shake our hands and toast a treaty.
The place is empty.'

'Lift your flasks to the King!
Fire the muskets!
Hail the empire's latest acquisition!
Terra Australis. Terra Nullius!'[5]

This stage is also connected to Australian Prime Minister Kevin Rudd's famous Sorry statement,[6] and the subsequent reconciliation marches across the country. After hearing about the dreadful stories of racism in the church, the desecration of the sacred Land at Maralinga, the genocide in country towns and the pollution of waters with poison, we came to realise that what we needed to do was more than apologies, sorry statements and rites of reconciliation,

In stage three, as our consciousness of the colonial curse grew, we became aware it was time for the churches to recognise that Abraham provided a serious precedent when he made a treaty with the Indigenous peoples of Canaan and affirmed their faith in *El*, the Creator Spirit of the Land of Canaan. The Abraham narrative provides a valid precedent for responding to *The Uluru Statement of the Heart*[7] by following the Abraham model and thereby advocating the implementation of the recommendations of this First Nations Australia peoples statement.

The Abraham precedent is articulated in detail in Uncle Norm's volume entitled *Acknowledgement of the Land and Faith of Aboriginal Custodians after Following the Abraham Trail*.[8] The Abraham legend in Genesis incorporates precolonial narratives that provide a biblical basis for the churches to endorse a treaty with First Nations Australia peoples and acknowledge their spiritual culture. In this text, he made the following statement:

---

5. Habel, *Reconciliation*, 169.
6. See Australian Parliament, 3 October 2008.
7. 2017 National Constitutional Convention; see ulurustatement.org for text.
8. Norman Habel, *Acknowledgement of the Land and the Faith of Aboriginal Custodians after Following the Abraham Trail* (Melbourne: Morning Star, 2018).

> It is time
> for the Christian churches in Australia
> to acknowledge publicly
> that frequently in the past
> they have dismissed
> the spirituality of First Nations Australia
> as worthless animism,
> and to acknowledge that we share
> a primal faith with Abraham and Sarah,
> and our First Nation friends,
> whether in Canaan or Australia
> or another pre-colonial country
> AND
> to declare publicly our commitment
> to help negotiate an Australian treaty
> in tune with
> the Uluru Statement from the Heart.[9]

The evolution of our colonial consciousness has not only led us to listen more closely to our First Nations Australia mentors, but also to challenge our approach to the field in which we have sometimes been regarded as an expert, namely, biblical interpretation. We began to ask how would/should our growing awareness of the colonial curse play a role in interpreting biblical texts?

Stage four commenced when Anne Pattel-Gray, a leading First Nations Australia scholar, challenged us to assist her to decolonise biblical narratives. Together we began the task of decolonising Genesis 1–11 and 12–25.

The initial outcome of this venture is two volumes entitled *Decolonising the Biblical Narrative*, Volumes 1 and 2, to be published in 2022 and 2023. The present volume will be volume 3 in this series.

One of the recurring issues we faced in decolonising these narratives was the recurrence of the name YHWH. The name YHWH is clearly an addition by a narrator of the biblical text of Genesis, since the name YHWH was only revealed to Moses, centuries later (Exod. 3.15). YHWH is an obvious addition, for example, in Genesis 15, where Abraham is promised a vast empire by YHWH even though Abraham does not know the name YHWH.

---

9. Habel, *Acknowledgement*, 73

These YHWH references led us to ask three questions:

• Who is this YHWH?
• Who is this God who promises colonial Lands?
• Is YHWH indeed a colonial God?

Our goal here is not to trace the ancient origin of the name YHWH itself.[10] Robert Crotty maintains that there is 'no conclusive evidence about the name of YHWH in cuneiform literature prior to the eighth century BC'.[11] However, in an unpublished study, Crotty suggests there is now evidence that YHWH was originally believed to be the progeny of *El*.

Our goal is to focus on the way the biblical narrator outlines the belief that the name, roles and character of YHWH are revealed to the people of Israel as recorded in the Book of Exodus.

There are numerous approaches to the interpretation of the narrative recorded in the Exodus text: theological, historical, literary critical, feminist, ecological and Christian. We contend now, with a growing colonial consciousness, that this biblical text is the work of a narrator who has collated narratives and traditions with a particular focus in mind: to reveal the name, role, character and will of YHWH to the future colonisers of the Land of Canaan.

The Decolonising Hermeneutic

YHWH, the name of the God that occurs some 6800 time in the Hebrew Scriptures, is hidden from the average reader because the name is usually translated 'Lord', as though it were a title rather than a name. This happened over the centuries because for many translators the name 'YHWH' was too sacred to be written and was replaced by Adonai, which means 'Lord'. As a result, the actual name YHWH was hidden from readers.

We have discovered that the name, identity, roles and character of YHWH are introduced by the narrator of the Book of Exodus in

---

10. William Albright, *Yahweh and the Gods of Canaan: A Historical Analysis of Two Contrasting Faiths* (New York: Doubleday Anchor, 1968); Mark Smith, *The Early History of God: Yahweh and Other Deities in Ancient Israel* (Grand Rapids: Eerdmans, 1990).

11. Robert Crotty, *Yahweh, the God of Israel* (Adelaide: Salisbury College of Advanced Education: Occasional Papers 14, 1976), 4.

progressive stages. While the name YHWH may have been viewed by some translators as too sacred to be identified in the text, the narrator of Exodus has no qualms about repeatedly announcing the specific name YHWH as the name of the God of Israel.

The methodology for our analysis of these portrayals of YHWH is the decolonising hermeneutic outlined in detail in Volume 1 of *Decolonising the Biblical Narrative*. The essentials of this approach include:

- **Suspicion one**: as we read the current Hebrew text, we suspect that most past translations and interpretations of the text reflect the orientation of readers in a contemporary colonial world, even though they may be unaware of their colonial orientation.
- **Suspicion two**: we also now suspect that the narrator of oral traditions may have edited ancient traditions in a way that made them relevant to his colonial context. For example, when God appears to Abraham to promise him the Land of Canaan (Gen 12:7), the narrator identifies God's name as YHWH even though YHWH is first revealed to Moses only centuries later (Exod 3:13–15).
- **Exposure**: as we identify evidence of a colonial worldview in the narrator's editing of these oral traditions, I believe we can expose not only the colonial language employed by the narrator but also a colonial version of a precolonial tradition.
- **Retrieval**: in some cases, it is also possible to retrieve a precolonial tradition embedded in the current colonial version.
- **Focus**: the task is not primarily to retrieve precolonial narratives— for example, the Ancestral Narratives retrieved from Genesis 1-11 in volume one of *Decolonising the Biblical Narrative* —but to focus on how the narrator of Exodus has traced the progressive stages in the revelation of YHWH as the colonial God of Israel.

Progressive Stages of Revelation

Discerning the role of the narrator is crucial for identifying the colonial dimensions of the text. The narrator is the colonial editor who has collated the relevant traditions and narrated them in language and thinking that reflects the colonial orientation of the narrator's cultural context.

In most theological circles, the God YHWH (Yahweh) in Exodus has been remembered as

- The mighty God of the Exodus who rescued the Israelites from slavery in Egypt
- The jealous God who made a personal covenant with the Israelites as Mt Sinai
- The amazing Lord God who revealed his bold presence and his divine will at Mt Sinai.

A close reading of the narratives of Exodus, taking into account the colonial worldview of the narrator, enables us to discern an underlying plan of the narrator to progressively outline the various stages in which the name, the roles and the character of the colonial God YHWH are revealed. These stages are summarised below.

- **The Anonymous God**
  In the precolonial narratives of Exodus 1 and 2, the God of the midwives (1:5) and the God who hears the groaning of Israel (2:24) remains anonymous.
- **The Unnamed God of the Fathers**
  The God who speaks to Moses out of the burning bush identifies himself as the God of Abraham, Isaac and Jacob (3:6), but no name is given for this God. Moses remains ignorant!
- **A God named, YHWH**
  Later, a frustrated Moses asks this God to reveal his name. This God then confesses that his name is YHWH (3:15).
- **The Canaanite God, *El Shaddai***
  After his initial cruel confrontations with Pharaoh, this God reveals to Moses that he appeared to Abraham, Isaac and Jacob as *El Shaddai,* the Creator God of Canaan (6:3).
- **A God who Overpowers Nature**
  The narrator then describes ten plagues that reveal the capacity of this God to overpower the forces of nature, everything from polluting the Nile to inundating the Land with hail and fire (Exod 7–11).
- **A God who Chooses his own People**
  This God, YHWH, then declares that of all the peoples on Earth, he has chosen Israel to be his own private possession (19:3–6), a privileged people who are obligated to obey his voice.

- **The Ominous Fire Cloud God**
  The God, YHWH, who has revealed his name, role and character to Moses, then makes a spectacular public appearance as a fire cloud (*kabod*) on top of Mt Sinai (19:16–18).
- **A Terrifying Colonial God**
  In the final stage, the climactic revelation, YHWH announces that he will not only enable Israel to colonise Canaan, but that he will send his 'terror' ahead to 'blot out' the Canaanites (23:23–33) and send his angel to 'drive out' all first nations in Canaan (33:2).

In the chapters that follow, we will analyse the relevant narratives of the Book of Exodus and demonstrate how the narrator reveals the roles and character of YHWH in the eight successive stages outlined above.

Cultural Context

Our interpretation reflects the current state of the evolution of our consciousness of the colonial curse and the decolonising hermeneutic that Anne Pattel-Gray and Uncle Norm have developed. The cultural context in which we both live is Australia, the Land of the First Nations peoples.

We are not interested in passing judgement on those who preceded us—biblical scholars, early settlers like our ancestors or committed missionaries. Each group's consciousness reflects the culture of their time and their perception of their task. Our concern for the environment, for example, moved us to develop an environmental hermeneutic which led us to read the plagues in Egypt as grey rather than green acts of God.

As Robert Kempe outlines in his response towards the end of this volume, the missionaries at Hermannsburg would not have believed that YHWH has given them to right to possess the Land, by whatever means. Their perceived their role was to reveal a compassionate God of love—not a cruel colonial God.

Our awareness of the significance of a cultural context in the interpretation process has changed in recent years. If we listen to First Nations Australia today, we realise that their cultural context—largely dismissed by colonial settlers—was ecological, communal and spiritual.

The cultural mindset of biblical scholars in the Western world has, in most cases, not been in sympathy with the cultural context of indigenous peoples throughout the world. Even the development of ecological hermeneutics did not stimulate serious research into the way First Nations Australia peoples read the landscape and lived as committed custodians of the Land.

Perhaps an even more significant factor is that until recently, biblical interpreters, had a limited awareness of the cultural context of the authors and editors of the books of the Bible. The task of the preacher and teacher was primarily to discern God's message in a given text rather than explore the particular focus of narrators in their individual cultural contexts.

We was aware that the Exodus narrative had many grey texts in which the country and creatures of Egypt were abused by the plagues,[12] but we had not appreciated—as Jione Havea indicates in his response in this volume—that the colonial God YHWH had not only abused nature but also the innocent Egyptian citizens. The people and the Land suffered because of the hard heart of Pharaoh—a heart that was hardened by the God YHWH.

We must now express our appreciation to George Rosendale, Anne Pattel-Gray and other First Nations mentors for giving me the knowledge and skills to recognise the cultural context of the narrator of the Book of Exodus—a text that we now read with a colonial consciousness.

---

12. Norman Habel, *An Inconvenient Truth: Is a Green Reading of the Bible Possible?* (Adelaide: ATF Press 2009), 16–19.

Chapter One
Moses and the Unidentified God

(Stage One)

---

*The account of how the narrator
progressively reveals the true character
of YHWH,
as the Colonial God of Israel,
commences with precolonial narratives
about how the children of Israel
had multiplied in Egypt,
but were forced to become slaves.
The midwives survived the oppression
by fearing a God
who is not identified
by the narrator
but is probably
El
the Creator Spirit of Abraham
and the Canaanites*

Bitter Oppression in Egypt Exodus 1:8–14

Oppression Under a New King

The narrative about the revelation of YHWH commences with a portrayal of the situation in Egypt when YHWH—after more than 400 years of Israelite slavery in Egypt—is finally about to reveal his presence and purpose. The situation is one of bitter oppression by the Egyptian taskmasters.

> Now there arose a new king over Egypt, who did not know Joseph. And he said to his people, 'Behold the people of Israel are too many and too mighty for us. Come, let us deal shrewdly with them, lest they multiply, and, if there is a war, they join our enemies and fight against us and escape from the land.'

> Therefore, they set taskmasters over them to afflict them with heavy burdens. And they built for Pharaoh store houses, Pithom and Ramses. But the more they were oppressed, the more they multiplied and the more they spread abroad.

The story of the Israelites in Egypt is divided into two eras: the period when Egyptian kings remembered Joseph and the blessings he brought to Egypt; the period after a new king arrived who did not know about Joseph. This Egyptian king appointed taskmasters and subdueed the Israelites. He was afraid that they would join the enemies of Egypt and escape from the Land.

The God of the Israelites remains anonymous in this part of the narrative until the narrator, later in the text, reveals the name and character of the God of the Israelites: YHWH.

Abandonment to Slavery

Even though the nature of the oppression is tantamount to slavery, the Israelites continued to multiply. The form of the slavery made the lives of the Israelite miserable.

The Egyptians were in dread of the people of Israel. So, they made the people of Israel serve with rigour, making their lives bitter with hard service, in mortar and brick, and in all kinds of work in the field. In all their work they made them serve with rigour.

Stage One

The God of the Midwives Exodus 1.15–22

Key Hebrew Term

- '*elohim*—the basic word for God, but not a reference to any specific God unless the name is given in the context; the God whom the midwives worship is not identified—probably quite deliberately—by the colonial narrator.

The Role of the Midwives

> Then the king of Egypt said to the Hebrew midwives, one of whom was named Shiphrah and the other Puah, 'When you serve as a midwife to the Hebrew women, and see them on the birthstool, if it is a son, you shall kill him; but if it is a daughter, she shall live'.

> But the midwives feared God and did not do as the king of Egypt commanded them, but let the male children live. So, the king of Egypt called the midwives and said to them, 'Why have you done this, letting the male children live?' The midwives said to Pharaoh, 'Because the Hebrew women are not like the Egyptian women. They are vigorous and are delivered before the the midwife reaches them.'

The precolonial heroes/heroines of this Exodus narrative are the Hebrew midwives. They not only serve as faithful midwives in a world of harsh slavery, they also have the courage and capacity to defy the Pharaoh, the King of Egypt. When commanded to kill male infants, they claim the Hebrew wives give birth to vigorous children they dare not kill.

Because the midwives are able to protect the male children, Pharaoh is angry and demands that the male children be thrown into the Nile where they will drown.

The God of the Midwives

> So, God dealt well with the midwives. The people multiplied and grew very strong. Because the midwives feared God, he gave them families. The Pharaoh commanded all the people 'Every son that is born to the Hebrews you shall throw into the Nile, but you shall let every daughter live'.

This precolonial narrative describes how the midwives were able to defy Pharaoh because they feared God. The narrator does not identify the God whom the midwives feared or the name of the God who dealt well with the midwives and enabled Israelite families to grow strong.

Why?

We suggest two possible related reasons. This narrative is a prelude to the stages in which the narrator reveals the name and character of YHWH in the text, and so naming this God in the narrative in Exodus 1:15–22 is premature as Moses claims he does not know the name of the God of the fathers (3:13).

A second reason for not naming this God is that the midwives probably feared El[1] —the God of their fathers who was also the God of the Canaanites. Even though much later, in Exodus 6.3, the narrator does identify the God of the fathers as the Canaanite God, *El Shaddai*, the narrator may have deliberately avoided referring to the God of the Canaanites as the source of the blessings bestowed on the midwives and the families they supported for cultural reasons.

Response

When we, along with First Nations Australia peoples, first hear the ancestral narrative of how the people of Israel were oppressed, abused and treated as slaves, we can sympathise with First Nations Australia who were treated as 'slaves' by the early colonial overlords.

How do we respond—as descendants of the colonial 'invaders'—when we discover that the God of the Australian settlers, who has oppressed the First Nations peoples of Australia, is the colonial God, YHWH, whose identity is revealed later in the Exodus narrative.

The identity of this God introduced by the Christian missionaries may not have been fully recognised in the days of early settlement because their God was simply designated 'Lord God'. This title, however, is actually a pious translation of the name of God revealed in Exodus: YHWH God.

A closer reading of the Exodus narrative, however, suggests that the God whom the midwives feared, while not named by the narrator, was probably El, the Creator Spirit of the Canaanites and the God of Abraham. If so, then we have in this narrative (1:15–22) a precedent for recognising the Creator Spirit of First Nations Australia.

This precedent has been recognised in *Acknowledgement of the Land and Faith of Aboriginal Custodians after Following the Abraham Trail* where Habel traces the faith of Abraham in Canaan and declares, the following:

---

1. Marvin Pope, *El in the Ugaritic Texts* (Leiden: Brill, 1955).

We settlers should now acknowledge publicly that we have dismissed Aboriginal beliefs in a Creator Spirit as paganism, unlike Abraham who recognised El, the Creator Spirit of the Indigenous Peoples of Canaan.[2]

Moses and the Groaning of the Israelites Exodus 2

The second precolonial narrative,
preserved by the narrator in anticipation
of the revelation of YHWH
as the colonial God of Israel,
is the famous legend about the survival
of Moses,
his flight to Midian
and
the unidentified God who finally
hears the Israelites groaning.

The Survival of Moses Exodus 2:1–10

Hiding Moses

The precolonial Moses legend commences with a story of how the future hero—the first Israelite to hear the name YHWH—survived the mandate of the Pharaoh to kill all male Hebrew children. The clever nuances of this ancestral legend, obviously retold many times orally, include how a basket made of bulrushes is hidden in the bulrushes of the famous Nile River.

> Now a man from the house of Levi took a daughter of Levi to be his wife. The woman conceived and bore a son. When she saw he was a fine baby she hid him for three months. When she could hide him no longer, she took a basket made of bulrushes and daubed it with bitumen and pitch. She placed the child in it and placed it among the reeds on the riverbank. The baby's sister stood some distance away to see what would happen to him.

---

2. Habel, *Acknowledgement*, 67.

When the daughter of Pharaoh finds the child, she adopts the baby as her son. This adoption means that Moses had royal status and great future potential as a son of the Pharaoh. One innuendo in the narrative asks what would have happened if Moses had become Pharaoh? By being raised as a son in the household of the Pharaoh, Moses nevertheless has the potential to become a leader.

His name, Moses, preserves the legend of his survival—a feature typical of precolonial ancestral narratives.

> Now the daughter of Pharaoh came down to bathe in the river while her maidens walked by the river. Then she saw the basket among the reeds and sent her maid to fetch it.

> When she opened it, she saw the child, and lo, the baby was crying. She took pity on him and said, 'This is one of the Hebrew babies'. Then his sister said to Pharaoh's daughter, 'Shall I go and call you a nurse from the Hebrew women to nurse the child for you?' And Pharaoh's daughter said to her, 'Go!' So, the girl went and called the child's mother. Then Pharaoh's daughter said to her, 'Take this child away and nurse him for me and I will give you your wages'.

> So, the woman took the child and nursed him. The child grew and later she brought him to Pharaoh's daughter, and he became her son. She named him Moses for she said, 'Because I drew him out of the water'.

Moses, the Murderer Exodus 2:11–15

The Murder

Even though Moses is raised as a son of the Pharaoh's daughter and would have experienced life as a member of the royal family, his Hebrew heritage rises to the surface when he sees an Egyptian beating a Hebrew.

> One day, when Moses was an adult, he went out to visit his people and saw their burden. He saw an Egyptian beating a Hebrew, one of his people. He looked this way and that and, seeing no one, he killed the Egyptian and hid him in the sand.

A precolonial tradition is preserved in the account of this incident: the act of murdering another human being would have been considered wrong—unless it was an Egyptian killing a slave. Yet, Moses—as an adopted Egyptian—is exonerated, even though he is made aware of his wrongdoing.

> When he went out next day, behold, two Hebrews were struggling together and he said to one man that he did wrong, 'Why did you strike this man?' He answered, 'Who made you a prince and judge over us? Do you mean to kill me as you killed the Egyptian?'
>
> Then Moses was afraid and thought, 'Surely this thing is known!' When Pharaoh heard of it he sought to kill Moses.

Moses does not escape his wrongdoing. His murder is known to his Hebrew brothers and his fate is apparently sealed once Pharaoh learns about the incident. Moses escapes to the land of Midian where the first crucial stage in the revelation of YHWH as the colonial God of Israel takes place.

Moses, the Sojourner Exodus 2:15–22

The Daughters of Midian

While being a sojourner in Midian, Moses encounters seven daughters of a priest named Reuel. Once again, the narrator does not identify the God whom this priest serves, even though he would obviously be a local God like the Canaanite God El that Abraham worshipped.

> Moses fled to the land of Midian and sat down by a well. The priest of Midian had seven daughter and they came to draw water. They filled their troughs to water their father's flock. The shepherds came to drive them away, but Moses stood up and helped them and watered their flock.
>
> When they came to Reuel their father, he said, 'How is it that you came home so soon today?' They said, 'An Egyptian delivered us out of the hands of the shepherds, and even drew water for us and watered our flock'. He said to his daughters, 'Where is he? Why have you left the man? Call him that he may eat bread.'

> Moses was content to dwell with the man, and he gave Moses
> his daughter Zipporah. She bore a son and he called his name
> Gershom. He said, 'I have been a sojourner in a foreign land!'

Moses befriends the seven women and protects them from the efforts
of local shepherds to take control of the well. Once again, women play
a crucial role in the precolonial narrative that precedes the revelation
of the colonial God of Israel.

The priest of Midian is then only too willing to welcome Moses—
just as Melchizedek, priest of Salem, welcomed Abraham when he
defended the local people of Canaan (Gen 14). The friendship even
extends to Moses marrying the daughter of a Midianite priest, clearly
a precolonial practice.

The Covenant in Canaan Exodus 2:23–25

The God who Hears Groaning

A change takes place in the progression of the narrative: after the
Pharaoh dies, their God finally hears the cry of the groaning Israelites.

After more than four hundred years, the unidentified God is
recorded as finally hearing the groaning of the people of Israel—a
compassionate God finally appears on the scene.

> Years later, the king of Egypt died. And the people of Israel
> groaned under their bondage and cried out for help. Their cry
> under bondage came to God.
>
> God heard their groaning and **God remembered his covenant**
> with Abraham, with Isaac and with Jacob. God saw the people
> of Israel and knew their condition.

Key Hebrew Terms

- *berit*—the traditional word for 'covenant' or 'treaty.' Which
  covenant God made with the patriarchs is not specified.
- *'elohim*—the basic word for God, but not a reference to any
  specific God unless the name is given in the context.

Who, then, is this compassionate God?

This God is not identified by the narrator as the God YHWH, who is yet to be revealed to Moses and Israel. Presumably this is El, the God of Abraham, the compassionate Creator Spirit of Canaan.

The Covenant Remembered

According to the present version of this narrative, this God remembers a covenant made with Abraham, Isaac and Jacob.

But which covenant is the narrator referring to?

The precolonial covenant that *El Shaddai*, the Creator Spirit of Canaan makes with Abraham (Gen. 17.1) or the colonial covenant made allegedly made between YHWH and Abraham (Gen. 15.18 and in later texts). If this is a precolonial text, the reference is to the original covenant between Abraham and El Shaddai, the Creator Spirit of Canaan.

If the narrator, in anticipation of his narrative about the revelation of YHWH as God of Israel, is hiding a reference to YHWH, then the narrator is playing games with a precolonial tradition.

Response

After listening to the experiences of First Nations Australia, we believe they could identify with the midwives who related personally to the Creator Spirit of the Indigenous peoples of Canaan and can respond positively to the same God who was compassionate with the groaning Israelites serving as slaves in ancient Egypt. As a Hebrew midwife we could relate positively to this precolonial God, who is apparently not the colonial God YHWH whose identity is revealed later in these narratives.

> *I am a Hebrew midwife*
> *who was expected to tend women*
> *about to give birth in ancient Egypt*
> *and to kill boy babies*
> *in response to the mandate of Pharaoh.*
> *I am proud to remember that we defied*
> *the Pharaoh and received the blessing*
> *of our Creator Spirit, El Shaddai,*
> *the God of our ancestors in Canaan.*

Chapter Two
The Unidentified God Reveals both Presence and Identity

(Stages Two and Three)

The account of how the narrator
progressively reveals the name and character
of YHWH, the Colonial God of Israel,
commences when Moses is confronted
with a presence
and a voice that claims to be
the God of Abraham, Isaac and Jacob.
When challenged by Moses
this God identifies himself
as
'YHWH, the God of your fathers'.

Stage Two

The God of Abraham Revealed Exodus 3:1–9

The God of your Father

The 'God of your father' is identified here as the God of Abraham, the God of Isaac and the God of Jacob—a God whose new name is unknown to Moses and is yet to be revealed.

> Now Moses was keeping the flock of his father-in-law, Jethro the priest of Midian. He led his flock to the west side of the wilderness and came to Horeb, the mountain of God.
>
> **The angel of YHWH appeared to him in a flame of fire**, out of the midst of a bush, but it was not consumed. Moses said, 'I will turn aside and see this great sight, why the bush is not burned'.

When YHWH saw he turned aside to see, God called to him out of the bush, 'Moses! Moses!' And Moses said, 'Here I am'. Then God said, 'Do not come near. Take off your shoes from your feet for the place on which you are standing is holy ground.'

Then God said, '**I am the God of your father**, the God of Abraham, the God of Isaac and the God of Jacob.' Moses hid his face for he was afraid to look at God.

Key Hebrew Terms

- *yahweh*—the name of the God YHWH, usually translated 'Lord' even though it is the name of the colonial God YHWH about to be revealed in stage three.
- *horeb*—the mountain of Horeb also known as Mt Sinai.
- *qodesh*—the term usually rendered holy, referring to places or items that are connected with God in some way.

The Burning Bush Presence

While Moses is acting as a shepherd for his father-in-law, he happens to be located near the holy mountain of Horeb—elsewhere identified as Sinai, the location of YHWH's spectacular manifestation in stage seven of the revelation sequence of events.

Suddenly, the presence of God is made manifest in mysterious flames of fire in a bush that is not consumed by the flames. This fiery presence anticipates the fire cloud of YHWH that appears later, on Mt Sinai. While this 'presence' is not yet identified, the narrator is employing classic symbols that anticipate the naming of this God as YHWH.

YHWH's presence is revealed in fire.

A God of Compassion

Moses is also informed, according to the narrator, that it was YHWH who then announces that he has seen the affliction of the people of Israel and heard their cries of anguish—even though Moses is still unaware of the name and role of YHWH.

> Then YHWH said, 'I **have seen the affliction of my people**
> and heard their cry because of their taskmasters. I have
> come to deliver them out of the hand of the Egyptians and to
> bring them out of that land to a good and broad land, a land
> flowing with milk and honey, to the place of the Canaanites,
> the Hittites, the Amorites, the Perizzites, the Hivites and the
> Jebusites. Behold the cry of the people of Israel has come to
> me and I have seen the oppression with which the Egyptians
> oppress them.

Significantly, the promise of YHWH is similar to the promise
delivered in his covenant with Abraham—a covenant edited by the
colonial narrator (Gen 15:17-21). The promise for the Israelites to be
able to colonise the land of Canaan and remove the peoples in that
land is not yet included in this promise that emphasises the plan of
this God to deliver the people of Israel out of the oppressive hands of
the Egyptians.

This promise is limited to bringing the Israelites to a land of milk
and honey. The colonial enterprise is not mentioned or implied.

The colonial intent of YHWH is yet to be revealed. The expression
of compassion for the Israelites in Egypt is not apparent, or explicit,
in the relationship of this God with any other peoples, such as the
Egyptians or Canaanites.

Stage Three
The Unidentified God Reveals a
New Identity Exodus 3:10–22

The Role of Moses

After his account of how the unidentified God reveals his presence—
but not his new name—to Moses and promises to rescue the Israelites
from slavery, the narrator focuses on the role of Moses in the rescue
operation. Without hesitation, the narrator makes explicit YHWH's
command.

> Come, I will send you to Pharaoh
> that you may bring forth my people
> the sons of Israel, out of Egypt.

Understandably, Moses' response demonstrates that he is aware of his problematic past, and is concerned about his own identity and safety. He does not yet know the identity of the God who is issuing commands from a bush that is on fire.

> Who am I that I should go to Pharaoh
> and bring the sons of Israel out of Egypt?

The response of the unidentified God anticipates the future revelation of this God on Mount Sinai where his *kabod*—his fiery presence—will also appear for all to see.

> I will be with you.
> And this will be the sign for you
> that I have sent you.
> When you have brought forth the people out of Egypt,
> **you will serve God on this mountain.**

Once again, the name of the God is not revealed.

Nevertheless, according to the narrator, Moses and his people will 'serve' this unidentified God on the mountain. The narrator has developed the plot so that pressure mounts on us—and Moses—to ask the name of this God. Finally, Moses asks the question.

> If I come to the people of Israel and say to them,
> 'The God of your fathers has sent me to you'
> and they ask me, '**What is his name?**'
> what shall I say to them?'
>
> God said to Moses: '**I AM WHO I AM!**
> Say this to the people of Israel,
> I AM has sent me to you.'

The Colonial Name Revealed

Once again, the narrator leaves us waiting for a clear identification of the God involved. The name 'I AM' is a cryptic anticipation of the name YHWH—a name that still leaves us wondering, Who is this God? The narrator then has the voice from the fire bush reveal the true name of this God who claims a long relationship with the people.

Say this to the people of Israel:
'YHWH, the God of your fathers,
the God of Abraham, Isaac and Jacob
has sent me to you.

This is my name for ever
and thus I am to be remembered
throughout all generations.

While the name of this previously unidentified God is now revealed as eternal, the significance of that name is yet to be specified. The narrator then records that Moses is commissioned to reveal the name and role of this newly identified God.

Go and gather the elders of Israel together
and say to them, '**YHWH, the God of your fathers,**
the God of Abraham, Isaac and Jacob
has appeared to me saying,
"I have observed you
and what has been done to you in Egypt.
I promise I will bring you
out of all the affliction of Egypt
to the land of the Canaanites...
a land flowing with milk and honey".

This identification of YHWH is pivotal in the underlying plan of the narrator.

- YHWH is revealed to be the name of this God
- YHWH claims to be the God of Israel's fathers
- YHWH plans to rescue the people of Israel from Egypt
- YHWH claims to have the power to smite Egypt
- YHWH promises to colonise the Israelites in Canaan.

The claim that YHWH is the God of Israel's fathers remains a mystery. We know from traditions preserved in Genesis that the name of God that the fathers knew in Canaan is *El*, variously now as *El Elyon*, El *Shaddai* and *El Olam*. Even though the narrator of the Abraham stories has Abraham communicating with YHWH, that name has only been revealed to Moses in the revelation process in the Book of Exodus.

Moses is also informed that the role of YHWH is not only to liberate his people from slavery, but also to fulfill the colonial covenant promise of providing land in Canaan for God's people.

The Role of YHWH in Egypt

The narrator outlines how the God YHWH will overcome the forces of Egypt in a way that anticipates the later colonial conquest of Canaan. Significantly, Moses is commissioned—first of all—to inform the king of Egypt that it is YHWH, the recently identified God of the Hebrews, who is addressing the Egyptian leadership. In the narrator's version, YHWH commands Moses:

> 'You and the elders of Israel
> shall go to the King of Egypt and say,
> **"YHWH, the God of the Hebrews,**
> has met with us and now we pray you,
> let us take a three-day journey into the wilderness,
> that we may sacrifice to YHWH, our God".'

The narrator continues the commission of YHWH to Moses by outlining what will happen in Egypt because of the powerful intervention of YHWH. This YHWH is depicted as acting in ways that reflect a fierce colonial character. The projected course of events includes:

- YHWH will use a 'mighty hand' to force the King of Egypt to grant the Israelites a three-day journey into the wilderness
- YHWH will smite Egypt with a mighty hand to force Pharoah to let the Israelites go
- YHWH will enable the women of the Israelite households to 'despoil' the Egyptian families by gathering silver, gold, and clothing.

Response

The revelation of a new God—or, at least a new name for God—recalls the missionaries' announcement that their God was a Trinity: Father God; Jesus Christ; Holy Ghost.

They did not, however, identify this God as the God of their 'fathers',[1] the spiritual ancestors of First Nations Australia. We also need to acknowledge that when First Nations Australia refers to their ancestors in their Ancestral Narratives, previously called Dreaming Narratives, there were both female and male ancestors.

Nor did they suggest that this new God heard the cries of agony experienced at the hands of European colonists.

The new God of the missionaries came to 'save us from our sins' not from the cruel treatment of the colonists, who were unaware that the Creator Spirit of First Nations Australia was similar to the Creator Spirit of Canaan, known to Abraham as El Shaddai, El Elyon and El Olam.

---

1. This term is italicised to emphasise that this is a patriarchal tradition that is still present for some Christian believers—a patriarchal perspective in many narratives in the Bible despite the Christian Scriptures efforts to underline the importance of women in Jesus' ministry and in some early Christian communities..

Chapter Three
Connecting with the God, *El Shaddai*

(Stage Four)

Before Moses has the courage
to confront Pharaoh
with the demand of YHWH
that Pharaoh
should set the Israelites free
to worship in the wilderness,
Moses is extremely anxious
and uncertain
until he gains the support of Aaron.

After they confront Pharaoh
the situation grows worse.
Moses then confronts YHWH
who reveals that his former identity
was indeed El Shaddai,
the Creator Spirit of Canaan.

The Trauma of Moses Exodus 4:1–31

Supportive Signs

Moses is depicted as being doubtful about his capacity to lead the Israelites out of Egypt into the wilderness. He expects his people will respond: YHWH did not appear to you!

In response, YHWH strengthens Moses' hand by providing three clever signs to verify his claims about the appearance of the recently identified God, YHWH. The first sign is a rod that turns into a serpent when thrown on the ground but becomes a rod when retrieved from the ground. This sign is to ensure that the people may 'believe that YHWH, the God of their fathers . . . has appeared to you'.

A second sign involves Moses inserting his hand into his bosom where it becomes white with leprosy only to be restored when removed from his bosom.

A third sign involves taking water from the Nile that turns into blood on the dry ground. Moses remains anxious, however, and claims he in not articulate enough to speak on behalf of YHWH.

> Moses said to YHWH,
> 'Oh, my Lord, I am not eloquent.
> I am slow of speech and of tongue.'
>
> Then YHWH said to him,
> 'Who made man's mouth?
> Who makes him dumb, or deaf or seeing or blind?
> **Is it not I, YHWH?**
> Now go, and I will be with your mouth
> and teach you what to say.'

Moses' anxiety about his capacity to be YHWH's spokesman, enables the narrator to reveal another dimension of the character of YHWH, namely, that he controls human capacities, a dimension that is extended in stage five when YHWH is portrayed as having control over all realms of nature.

The Intervention of Aaron

Moses' unwillingness to automatically obey YHWH's commission angers YHWH.

YHWH suggests Moses asks Aaron to speak instead.

> Is there not Aaron, your brother, the Levite?
> I know he can speak well
> and behold, he is coming out to meet you.
>
> He will speak for you to the people
> and he will be a mouth for you
> and **you will be to him as God.**

After receiving this promise from YHWH, Moses takes his leave from Jethro, his father-in-law, only to be informed by YHWH: **I will harden the heart of Pharaoh so that he will not let the people go.**

Despite Moses' anxiety in response to YHWH's words, YHWH then informs him of the cruel and murderous intentions of the brutal colonial God of Israel:

> You shall say to Pharaoh,
> 'Israel is my firstborn son, and I say to you,
> Let my son go that he may serve me.
> If you refuse to let him go,
> behold, I will slay your firstborn.'

The apparent compassion of YHWH for the Israelites is balanced by an unequivocal readiness to treat the Egyptian Pharoah with blatant violence and colonial cruelty.

The Response of the Elders

Aaron takes Moses into the wilderness near the mountain of God. Here they gather the elders of the people of Israel. Aaron convinces them that the God YHWH has indeed spoken to Moses and that they should believe Moses.

> And the people believed,
> when they heard that
> **YHWH had visited the people of Israel**
> and that he had seen their affliction,
> they bowed their heads
> and worshipped.

Even though the people of Israel had never heard of YHWH, they are portrayed as followers willing to worship a new God.

The Response of Pharaoh Exodus 5:1–21

YHWH Confronts Pharaoh

Moses and Aaron confront Pharaoh with the word of YHWH and face the implicit consequences if he refuses to obey.

> Moses and Aaron went to Pharaoh and said,
> 'Thus saith YHWH, the God of Israel,
> **Let my people go,**
> that they may hold a feast for me
> in the wilderness.'

Understandably, Pharaoh responds by revealing his ignorance about YHWH, and refuses to obey the command to let the people of Israel go.

> Pharaoh said, '**Who is YHWH,**
> that I should heed his voice and let Israel go?
> I do not know YHWH
> and I will not let Israel go!'

Pharaoh then ordered the taskmasters to make the labour of the Israelites more arduous. They forced the Israelites to find their own straw to make the same number of bricks.

However, the Egyptian foremen became disgruntled because of Pharaoh's harsh demands. They met with Moses and Aaron and explicitly threaten them in the name of YHWH. Significantly, the foremen did not threaten Moses and Aaron in the name of an Egyptian God, but with a measure of sarcasm called on this new and unknown God to judge them.

> YHWH look upon you and judge,
> because you have made us offensive
> in the sight of Pharaoh and his servants
> and have put a sword in their hands to kill us.

Identification with *El Shaddai* Exodus 5:22–6:9

The Complaint of Moses

The crisis Moses faces in response to the agony of his own people and the retaliation of the Egyptian foremen forces Moses to accuse YHWH of bringing evil upon the people of Israel.

> Then Moses turned to YHWH again and said,
> **'Why have you done evil to this people?**
> Why did you ever send me?
> Since I came to Pharaoh and speak in your name,

he has done evil to this people
and you have not delivered your people at all!'

The prelude to the fourth stage in the revelation of the role and character of YHWH is a crisis that provokes Moses to accuse YHWH of causing his people's misery. The courage of Moses is a catalyst that leads to the subsequent revelation of YHWH as being one with *El Shaddai*. YHWH responds to Moses' accusation by making this surprising declaration.

> YHWH said to Moses,
> 'Now you will see what I will do to Pharaoh.
> With a strong hand he will send them out.
> Yes, with a strong hand
> he will drive them out of this land.'

The Connection with *El Shaddai*

Rather than report on how YHWH will be involved in forcing Pharaoh to drive the Israelites out of the land, the narrator unveils an unexpected revelation about the identity of YHWH.

> God said to Moses, '**I am YHWH.**
> I appeared to Abraham, to Isaac and to Jacob
> **as El Shaddai.**
> But by the name YHWH
> I did not make myself known to them.

Stage four in the revelation of the name, role and character of YHWH is a surprise and significant. Why?

- YHWH has already been associated by the narrator with the God of Abraham, but his true name has remained hidden
- To identify YHWH as one and the same God as *El Shaddai* implies a hidden association with the Creator Spirit of Canaan
- The name YHWH was not known to the patriarchs even though the colonial narrator of the Genesis narratives claims YHWH did communicate with Abraham.

Many scholars have explored the origin and revelation of the formula 'I AM YHWH' assuming a theological reflection about the nature of God permeating the text. Zimmerli maintains that a 'fully conscious theological reflection has placed the formula precisely here first. It cannot appropriately appear any earlier, nor can it appropriately go silent now that it has appeared.[1]

While there may clearly be an alleged theological dimension involved in revealing the divine name YHWH at this stage in the narrative, in the wider orientation of the narrator, the revelation of the name of YHWH also anticipates the colonial plan to be revealed to Moses and the Israelites. The formula 'I AM YHWH' is also a symbol of the colonial dimension of this God's plan and character.

The God *El* is the Creator God of Canaan, variously identified in Genesis as *El Shaddai*, *El Elyon* and *El Olam*. The God *El* is not a celestial God but associated with the Land and the Canaanite peoples of the Land.[2] In Genesis 15.19, *El* is portrayed as 'Maker of sky and land'. This specific character of *El*, however, is not embraced in the sequence of revelations by the colonial narrator of Exodus.

The connection with *El Shaddai*, suggested by the narrator, is found in the covenant made with the patriarchs,

> **I established my covenant with them,**
> **to give them the land of Canaan,**
> the land in which they dwelt as sojourners.
> I have heard the groaning of the people of Israel
> whom the Egyptians hold in bondage
> and I have remembered my covenant.
>
> **I am YHWH!**
> I will bring you out from under
> the burdens of the Egyptians
> and I will deliver you from their bondage.

As indicated earlier, the reference to the covenant with the patriarchs is problematic. Which covenant is referred to: the covenant between Abraham and *El Shaddai* (Gen 17:1–2) or the covenant with YHWH inserted by the colonial narrator (Gen 15:18)?

The specific covenant with *El Shaddai*, the Creator Spirit of Canaan, is a promise of future progeny and a promise that *El Shaddai* would be their God forever in the land of Canaan (Gen 17:8).

---

1. Walther Zimmerli, *I Am Yahweh* (Atlanta: John Knox Press, 1982), 7.
2. Pope, *El*, 52; Habel, *Acknowledgement*, 23.

The alternative covenant with YHWH in Genesis 15 is a colonial promise that the descendants of Abraham will possess a vast territory from the Nile in Egypt to the Euphrates in Babylon. The Exodus narrator seems to associate a colonial vision with the covenant with *El Shaddai*, even if that was not the included in the explicit primary intent of the covenant made in Genesis 17.

> Say, therefore to the people of Israel,
> **'I am YHWH**
> and I will bring you out
> from under the burdens of the Egyptians.
>
> I will take you for my people
> and I will be your God
> and you shall know that
> **I am YHWH, your God**
> who has brought you out
> from under the burden of the Egyptians.
>
> I will bring you to the land
> I swore to give to Abraham, Isaac and Jacob.
> I will give it to you as a possession.
> **for I am YHWH!'**

A striking addition to the identification of YHWH with *El Shaddai* is the claim of YHWH that the people will know not only that YHWH has kept the promise to the patriarchs, but also that the God YHWH is indeed their God who delivered them from the burdens imposed by the Egyptians.

The rescue of Israel from the Egyptians, however, will also enable the colonial YHWH to eventually give the Israelites colonial possession of the land of Canaan.

This new promise, however, does not convince the people of Israel that YHWH could liberate them from their Egyptian oppressors.

> Moses spoke thus
> to the people of Israel,
> **but they did not listen to Moses,**
> because of their broken spirit and
> their cruel bondage.

Response

It is significant that the God of the Israelites in Egypt claims to be formerly known by Abraham as *El Shaddai*, the Creator Spirit of the indigenous peoples of Canaan. In addition, the character of El Shaddai resonates with the character of the Creator Spirit of the First Nations people in Australia, a Creator Spirit variously known as *Biame*, Rainbow Spirit, *Wandjina* and *Yiirmbal*.[3]

It is alarming, however, that the God of the Israelites in Egypt reveals that his real name is YHWH and that his true identity is that of a God whose intention is to enable the Israelites to steal and colonise the land of *El Shaddai*, the Creator Spirit of Canaan, the God Abraham recognised.

We can applaud the promise to rescue the Israelites from the oppressive taskmasters of Egypt, but we are appalled that the ultimate outcome is to take 'possession' of the land of the God *El Shaddai*. 'Possession' does not imply making a treaty with the peoples of Canaan as Abraham had done.[4]

> *It is time to accept*
> *that the God of Abraham*
> *was not named YHWH,*
> *the later God of the Israelites,*
> *but EL, the Creator Spirit of the land*
> *of the Canaanites,*
> *who were not godless savages.*
> *It is time to acknowledge*
> *that the European settlers did not*
> *respect the First Nations*
> *people of this land*
> *and their Creator Spirit,*
> *the way that Abraham recognised*
> *the Creator Spirit*
> *of First Nations Canaan.*

---

3. Rainbow Spirit Elders, *Rainbow Spirit Theology*, 31.
4. Habel, *Acknowledgement*, 28.

Chapter Four
A God who Overpowers Nature

(Stage Five)

According to the narrator,
YHWH,
the God of the Israelites,
has the power to control
the forces of nature
in such an unnatural way
as to finally force
Pharaoh
to let the Israelites
go into the wilderness
to serve YHWH
and finally
to divide the sea
into two walls of water
so that the Israelites could escape,
the Egyptians could be drowned
and YHWH be acclaimed
a victorious warrior God.

A Rescue Plan Against Nature Exodus 8–11

The First Plague

The first plague announces that the plagues are designed specifically to reveal to Pharaoh that it is YHWH who is demanding that Pharaoh liberate the people of Israel. Even though Pharaoh's heart has been hardened by YHWH, Moses is commissioned to visit Pharaoh early in the morning.

YHWH, the God of the Hebrews
sent me to you
saying 'Let my people go,
that they may serve me in the wilderness.
Behold, you have not obeyed!'

Thus says YHWH,
'By this you shall know that
I AM YHWH!
Behold I will strike the water in the Nile
with the rod that is in my hand
and it shall be turned into blood.

The fish in the Nile shall die
and the Nile shall become foul
and the Egyptians will be loath to drink
water from the Nile.

The first plague is an ugly work of YHWH that illustrates a willingness to violate the normal laws of nature to achieve the ultimate goal of liberating Hebrew people from Egypt, as does YHWH's 'hardening' of Pharaoh's heart. YHWH's commitment to free the Israelite is so relentless that YHWH shows no sympathy for the people of Egypt— or for the creatures on the land or in the Nile.

And YHWH said to Moses 'Say to Aaron,
"Take your rod and stretch out you hand
over the waters of Egypt,
over the rivers, their canals and their ponds,
all their pools of water that they may become blood.
There shall be blood throughout the land of Egypt
both in vessels of wood and in vessels of stone".

This text relating to the action of Aaron casting his rod over the waters of the Nile has been identified as a 'grey' text rather than a 'green' text. The God is not sustaining a life-giving force but creating a destructive force in relation to nature.[1]

---

1. Habel, *An Inconvenient Truth*, 18.

The Twelve Plagues

All the plagues are designed to demonstrate the same power: the colonial power of YHWH manipulating nature to force Pharaoh to liberate Israel—even though Pharaoh's refusal is due to YHWH's hardening his heart, making him incapable of acting in any other way. The process of 'hardening the heart' is tantamount to abusing a force of nature and seems to reflect a measure of revenge in the attitude of YHWH.

Plague 1: Blood pollutes the Nile and the Land; all fish in the Nile die and no water is suitable for drinking.

Plague 2: Frogs inundate not only the Nile but also the private homes of all the people of Egypt, spreading the pollution begun in the Nile.

Plague 3: Gnats arise from the dust to attach themselves to humans and animals.

Plague 4: Swarms of flies invade not only the houses of the Egyptians and their servants but also the ground until the Land of Egypt is ruined.

Plague 5: All the animals of the Egyptians are killed by the hand of YHWH while the animals of the Israelites survive—an action that again hardens Pharaoh's heart so that he does not even permit the Israelites to take a three-day journey into the wilderness to make sacrifices to YHWH.

Plague 6: A toxic dust that Moses throws into the air causes sores to break out on all Egyptians and all their animals.

Plague 7: Pestilence.
After the sixth plague, YHWH announces that future plagues will actually be 'plagues upon your hearts' so that when the pestilence strikes the Egyptians are allowed to survive. Why?

> For this purpose,
> I have let you live
> **to show you my power**
> so that my name [YHWH]
> may be declared
> throughout all the land.

Plague 8: Hail is sent by YHWH when Pharaoh still prevents the Israelites taking leave to sacrifice in the wilderness.

Plague 9: Thunder, hail and fire are sent down to destroy everything on the Land including every plant and every tree. When the thunder, hail and fire cease, YHWH again hardens Pharaoh's heart.

Plague 10: Locusts are then sent by the East wind to cover the face of the Land with darkness and consuming any fruit left on the trees.

Plague 11: Total darkness is imposed on all the Land preventing the Egyptians from seeing one another, but not affecting the lives of the Israelites.

In anticipation of the final plague—the killing of the first-born sons of the Egyptians—each Israelite family is commanded to gather in their father's house to celebrate a communal meal which came to be known as the 'Passover' even though the original meaning is probably 'Stand Guard Over' because YHWH promises to stand guard over each family that has placed blood on the doorposts to ward off the angel of death. As Moses said,

> YHWH will pass through to slay the Egyptians,
> and when he sees the blood on the lintel
> and on the two doorposts,
> **YHWH will stand guard** over the door
> and will not let the Destroyer enter your houses
> to slay you.
> You shall observe this rite as an ordinance
> for you and your sons forever.
> **When you come to the land**
> **which YHWH shall give you as he promised,**
> you shall keep this service.

At midnight, according to the narrator, YHWH smote all the innocent firstborn in the Land of Egypt, from the firstborn of Pharaoh who sat on the throne to the firstborn of the cattle.

Plague 12: The first-born sons of all the Egyptian families and the first-born of their cattle are killed and a cry goes out into all the Land.

But inexplicably, YHWH hardens Pharaoh's heart again.

Finally, the outcry of the Egyptian people forces Pharaoh to summon Moses and Aaron.

> Rise up, go forth from among my people,
> both you and the people of Israel.
> Go serve YHWH as you have said.
> Take your flocks and your herds as you have said
> and be gone. Bless me also.

After YHWH slaughters all the innocent first-born of the Egyptians and their cattle in the Land of Egypt, the Israelites leave for the desert. The narrator claims there were six hundred thousand men as well as women and children. The Israelites had been in Egypt for four hundred and thirty years.

The Israelites, led by YHWH, initially camped at Etham on the edge of the wilderness.

> YHWH went before them in a pillar of clouds
> to lead them along the way
> and by night in **a pillar of fire**
> to give them light,
> that they might travel by day and by night.

The presence of YHWH is again evident by a fire cloud; YHWH's association with fire is first revealed to Moses in the burning bush and later, the clouds of fire reveal 'YHWH' presence on Mt Sinai.

Though YHWH continues to inform Moses where to travel, once again—perhaps mysteriously as the explicit goal seems to have been achieved—hardens Pharaoh's heart so that he pursues the Israelites. YHWH explicitly reveals the ultimate goal of the rescue plan: 'I will get glory over Pharaoh and all his host and the Egyptians shall know that **I am YHWH**'.

The expression 'get glory over' is a verbal form of the noun *kabod*— the spectacular 'fire cloud' that reveals YHWH's presence on Mt Sinai in stage seven. Only now does YHWH reveal that all the acts of divine intervention are designed to not only to rescue the Israelites but also, especially, to reveal the presence and destructive power of YHWH.

The stunning events associated with the crossing of the Red Sea and the actual exodus of the Israelites from their slavery in Egypt reveal that YHWH is a unique God who can interrupt the normal course of nature to demonstrate relentless power and overpowering presence and control over all creation.

Moses assures the Israelites that YHWH is indeed the power that will be their salvation.

> And Moses said to the people,
> 'Fear not! Stand firm!
> **See the salvation**
> YHWH will work for you today.
> The Egyptians you see today
> you will never see again.
> **YHWH will fight** for you
> and you have only to be still.'

The pillar of cloud and darkness separated the Israelites from the Egyptian host until YHWH reveals another spectacular intervention in the morning—a powerful act of ultimate rescue from the threat of the pursuing Egyptian army.

> Moses stretched out his hand over the sea,
> and **YHWH drove the sea back**
> by a strong East wind all night
> and made the sea dry land
> and the waters were divided.

The division of the waters enabled the Israelites to cross on dry ground with a wall of water to their right and dry Land to their left. When the Egyptians tried to follow their chariots became clogged in the mud.

YHWH now tells Moses to stretch out his hand once more and make the waters join again so that the Egyptians are inundated with waters until they are all drowned. According to the narrator, this is another intervention by their powerful God YHWH.

> **YHWH saved Israel**
> from the hand of the Egyptians,
> and the Israelites saw the Egyptians dead
> on the seashore.
> Israel saw the great work that YHWH did
> against the Egyptians.

The people feared YHWH
and believed in YHWH
and in his servant Moses.

It is understandable that in the light of the overpowering works of YHWH—fighting and destroying the Egyptians by intervening in the forces of nature—that the song of celebration by Moses and the people declares that '**YHWH is a man of war. YHWH is his name**' (Exod 15:3).

YHWH is revealed to be a God, not only with the overwhelming capacity of a great warrior to rescue the people, but to intervene in the courses of nature in cruel ways that are contrary to the laws of nature.

Response

The portrayal of YHWH as a God who can manipulate nature is indeed spectacular. Among the First Nations peoples of Australia, the Creator Spirit is in tune with nature and enables the First Nations peoples to be custodians of the Land. The character of YHWH as lord over nature—rather than a Creator Spirit that animates nature—is problematic for First Nation Australia. From a First Nations perspective, YHWH abuses nature to liberate his people.

First Nations Australia would not even consider the possibility that the God YHWH would manipulate nature to rescue them from the colonial curse. There is no kinship between the colonial God YHWH and the Creator Spirit in this Land.

Chapter Five
The God who Colonises Nations and Appears in Person

(Stages Six and Seven)

According to the narrator,
at a camp near Mt Sinai,
the relationship of YHWH to the Israelites
and their role in the future
involves two special revelations
relating to YHWH.
YHWH chooses one people
to be his personal possession,
his colony nation,
one from among all nations
on Earth.
YHWH then reveals
his unique presence
as a fire cloud
in their presence.

Stage Six
The Personal Possession of YHWH Exodus 19:1–6

The Conquest by YHWH

After a series of interactions with his father-in-law, Jethro (Exod 18), following YHWH's lead, Moses takes his people to the wilderness of Sinai (Exod 19) and camps near the mountain where the cloud of YHWH's presence rests: Mt Sinai.

YHWH tells Moses to remind the people of Israel of YHWH's spectacular achievement at the Red Sea: the conquest and destruction of the Egyptian army as they crossed the Red Sea intent of taking them the people back to Egypt. The Israelites owe their liberation to their great and powerful God YHWH.

> You shall say to the house of Jacob
> and tell the people of Israel:
> 'You have seen what I did to the Egyptians
> and how I bore you on eagle's wings
> and **brought you to myself**.

The reference to 'myself' anticipates that Israel can expect not only to hear the voice of YHWH but also to experience the very Presence of YHWH, the fire cloud.

The Colonial Covenant

YHWH then announces a new covenant: the people of Israel are expected to obey the voice of YHWH. If so, they will then be chosen to be YHWH's personal possession and become the holy colonial nation of YHWH.

> Now, therefore,
> if you will obey my voice
> and keep my covenant,
> **you shall be my own possession**
> **among all peoples**
> for all the Earth is mine.
> You shall be to me a kingdom of priests
> and a holy nation.

In order to be faithful to this covenant, YHWH reveals that the people of Israel need to obey their God's voice and ordinances. These laws are outlined later, first in the so-called Ten Commandments (Exod 20) and subsequently in a wider range of ordinances (Exod 21–23).

What makes this conditional covenant significant is that YHWH is announcing that the obedient people of Israel with become

- a personal possession—a colonial nation and the colonial property—of YHWH
- chosen by YHWH from all the peoples on Earth
- a kingdom of people that can relate to YHWH as priests
- a nation that is distinctive/holy among all nations.

YHWH's choosing the Israelites as personal property and a priestly nation makes all other peoples on Earth secondary and without direct communication with YHWH. To become the personal property of YHWH is tantamount to becoming YHWH's treasured colony.

Stage Seven
The Visible Revelation of YHWH as
Celestial Fire Exodus 19:7–19

Announcing the Fire Cloud

The Israelites agree to obey the voice of YHWH after Moses announces details of the colonial covenant. In response, YHWH announces to Moses, 'Lo, I am coming to you in a thick cloud that the people may hear when I speak with you and also believe you forever'.

The appearance of the fire cloud on Sinai is not a secondary, but a visible confirmation of the colonial covenant announced by Moses; as a consequence Moses' word becomes the word of YHWH.

The Israelites are expected to consecrate themselves for three days in preparation for the appearance of the fire cloud of YHWH for all the people to see. Moses prepares them for the revelation of their God.

> Be ready by the third day,
> for on the third day
> YHWH
> will come down on Mt Sinai
> in the sight of all the people.

The Appearance of the Fire Cloud

After consecrating the people of Israel for three days, the fire cloud— revealing YHWH's presence—appears with spectacular visual and loud signs of their God's presence on Mt Sinai.

> On the morning of the third day,
> there were thunders and lightnings
> and a thick cloud upon the mountain.
> There was a very loud trumpet blast
> and all the people in the camp trembled.
> Then Moses took the people out of the camp

> to meet God.
> They took their stand at the foot of the mountain.
> Mt Sinai became wrapped in smoke
> because **YHWH descended upon it in fire!**
>
> And the smoke of it went
> like the smoke of a kiln
> and the whole mountain quaked heavily.
>
> As the sound of the trumpet grew louder
> Moses spoke and God answered him in thunder.
>
> **YHWH came down upon Sinai**
> to the top of the mountain.
>
> YHWH called Moses to the top of the mountain
> and Moses went up.

The thunder, lightning and trumpets are but preparation for the appearance of YHWH as celestial fire descending into the cloud and onto the mountain.

In Exodus 19, YHWH is portrayed, in a legend employed by the narrator, as fire in a cloud—a Presence of Israel's God often designated as the *kabod* of YHWH, a term frequently translated 'glory', as for example in Isaiah 6.3.

Ten Colonial Commandments (20:1–20)

The people and the priests are not permitted to accompany Moses up the mountain and into the fire presence of YHWH.

In YHWH's presence on Mt Sinai, Moses, receives the so-called Ten Commandments, the formulation that reveals additional dimensions of the character of YHWH as the colonial God of Israel. The commandments are introduced with the assurance that these commandments are given by YHWH, the God of the Exodus and the God of the colonial covenant.

> God spoke all these words saying,
> **I am YHWH your God**
> who brought you
> out of the Land of Egypt,
> out of the house of bondage.

The first two commandments reflect the bold claim of YHWH, that, for the Israelites, YHWH is the only God to be recognised in person or as an image.

> You shall have
> no other gods
> beside me.
> You shall not make
> for yourselves
> a graven image.

These two commandments are followed by a declaration that reflects the relentless approach of YHWH—a jealous attitude that compliments their God's colonial character.

> **I am YHWH your God, a jealous God,**
> who visits the iniquity of the fathers
> upon the children
> to the third and fourth generation
> of those who hate me,
> but showing steadfast love
> to thousands of those who love me
> and keep my commandments.

Obedience to the demands of YHWH's colonial covenant is unequivocal. Israel may be the chosen nation of YHWH, but its future is totally dependent upon conformity to the commands of the covenant.

> You shall not take
> the **name of YHWH,**
> **your God**, in vain.
> Remember the sabbath day
> to keep it holy.

The next commandment is more than a call to respect one's parents. Honouring one's ancestors ensures that the nation of Israel will be able to continue on the Land where their colonial God, YHWH, will facilitate their continuous settlement.

> Honour your father and mother,
> that your days
> may be long on the Land that
> **YHWH, your God,**
> gives you.

The remaining commandments seem to be positive guidelines that may well be precolonial commandments that have not been modified by the colonial narrator.

> You shall not kill.
> You shall not steal.
> You shall not commit adultery.
> You shall not bear false witness
> against your neighbour.
> You shall not covet anything
> that is your neighbour's.

The Israelites are terrified when they experience the thunder and lightning, and a smoking mountain. In fear, they plead with Moses.

> 'You speak to us and we will hear,
> but let God not speak to us or we will die.'

> And Moses said,
> 'Do not fear, for God has come to prove to you
> that the fear of him may be before your eyes,
> that you may not sin.'

YHWH's revelation on Mt Sinai and choosing Israel is not only a spectacular Presence, but also a terrifying Presence.

In stage seven of the revelation of the nature of the God YHWH in the Book of Exodus, to 'fear God' is not a pious expression of dutiful obedience that facilitates wisdom (as in Prov. 1.7); it involves an overwhelming dread that demands total obedience.

To 'fear YHWH' is to be aware of YHWH's terrifying Presence as a colonial God. The fear of the Lord (YHWH) is not the beginning of wisdom, but the fear of punishment.

Response

For First Nations Australia peoples, the Creator Spirit is not a terrifying Presence imposing fear from the top of a mountain. The Creator Spirit is a spiritual presence rising from the Land to communicate how to live as custodians of the Land.

For First Nations Australia, our Ten Commandments would relate to the Land as our spiritual source.

> *You shall celebrate the presence of*
> *the Creator Spirit rising from the Land.*

> *You shall recognise the Land*
> *as the home of all spirit beings.*

> *You shall read the landscape*
> *to learn how to live on the Land.*

> *You shall remember your calling*
> *to be custodians of the Land.*

> *You shall honour your ancestors*
> *and all your kin in the Land.*

> *You shall celebrate your bond with the Land*
> *at sites alive with spiritual presence.*

Even though YHWH the Colonial God gave the Israelites the 10 Commandments:

> You shall not kill.
> You shall not steal.
> You shall not commit adultery.
> You shall not bear false witness.
> against your neighbour.
> You shall not covet anything that is your neighbour's

Australia's First Nations peoples saw very early the hypocrisy of the British invading colonisers because they preached the 10 commandments to Aboriginal people while at the same time, they broke even commandment that YHWH demanded they follow. The British Coloniser stole the land from Australia's First Nations people, they massacred thousands of Aboriginal men, women, and children, they kidnapped generations of children and raped children and women. Even today, the Christian Churches still failed to see these historical lies or their failure to speak truth into this context today.

Chapter Six
A Terrifying Colonial God called YHWH

(Stage Eight)

According to the narrator,
the God called YHWH
announces his intention
not only to bring his people
to settle in Canaan,
but also to enable
the Israelites to remove
the peoples of Canaan
and to possess the Land of Canaan
as their exclusive Land
by employing ruthless techniques,
including revealing their God's **'Terror'**,
by sending hornets,
and forcing the Canaanites
to turn their backs on their Land
like cowards.

Keeping the Covenant Exodus 21:1–23:22

After announcing the Ten Colonial Commandments, Moses receives almost one hundred ordinances that demonstrate how the people of Israel are to experience life in the Land to which YHWH will take them. These ordinances include many things including

- buying a Hebrew slave
- selling a daughter as a slave
- striking a slave
- cursing a parent

- stealing an ox
- seducing a virgin
- lying with a beast
- afflicting a widow
- uttering false reports.

This collage of commandments concludes with a promise that an angel will accompany the people of YHWH to guard them on their way to the Land prepared for them by YHWH.

> Behold, I send an angel before you
> to guard you on the way
> and bring you to the place
> I have prepared.
> Give heed to him and hearken to his voice.
> Do not rebel against him,
> for he will not pardon your transgression.
> **My name is in him!**
> But if you hearken attentively
> to his voice
> and do all that I say,
> then I will be
> an enemy to your enemies and
> an adversary to your adversaries.

The angel of YHWH is a special manifestation of the voice and presence of YHWH as the Israelites prepare to travel to the Land that their colonial Landlord has prepared for them. If the people obey the voice of the angel of YHWH, YHWH will protect them. This reference begins to reveal the militant character of YHWH—a dimension revealed in detail in the colonial promises that follow.

Also significant is that the very name YHWH is a frightening factor to be faced by any adversary since the very name YHWH is in the angel accompanying the people. Perhaps this is an implicit reason that some translators chose to render the name YHWH as `adonai, meaning 'lord', rather than use the militant name of YHWH.

Blotting Out the Canaanites Exodus 23:23–26

The colonial character of YHWH is blatantly obvious in YHWH's promises—notably that all First Nations peoples of the Land of Canaan are to be blotted out as if they were vermin.

When the angel goes before you and brings you to
the Hittites, the Perizzites,
the Canaanites, the Hivites and the Jebusites
I will blot them out!
You shall not bow down to their Gods,
nor serve them
nor do according to their works
but you shall utterly overthrow them
and break their pillars in pieces.
You shall serve YHWH, your God
and I will bless your bread and your water.
I will take sickness away from your midst.
None of you shall cast your young
or be barren in your Land.
I will fulfill the number of your days.

There is no appreciation of the spiritual culture or contribution of the Canaanites to the welfare of Canaan, a 'land flowing with milk and honey' (*cf* Deut 6:10–12). There is no acknowledgement that Abraham had a harmonious relationship with members of the Canaanite community and worshipped their Creator Spirit.

If the Israelites serve YHWH faithfully, after YHWH has destroyed all former inhabitants of the Land given to them for their exclusive use, they will enjoy a prosperous life in the Land of Canaan—a life free from sickness.

YHWH, the colonial God of Israel, has the future of the Israelite people exclusively in mind. Other peoples are irrelevant and disposable.

The Terror of YHWH Exodus 23:26–29

The Israelites are assured that their God, YHWH, will employ ruthless techniques to remove the peoples of Canaan from the Land of Canaan. Terror (`*eymar*) and dread are experienced in the presence of the Warrior God, YHWH (Exod. 15.16).

I will send my terror before you
and throw into confusion
all the people against whom you shall come.
I will make all your enemies
turn their backs to you.

> **I will send hornets** before you and drive out
> Hivite, Canaanite and Hittite from before you.
> I will not drive them out in one year
> lest the Land become desolate
> and wild beasts multiply against you.

The process of 'blotting out' the inhabitants of the land of Canaan is here described is terms of frightening acts of divine intervention. While the 'terror' of the colonial God, YHWH, may remain something of a mystery, it clearly reflects the ruthless character of YHWH. The use of hornets is less cruel, but nevertheless devastating. That YHWH causes the Canaanites to turn their backs implies YHWH is turning them into cowards rather than real enemies.

Colonising the Land Exodus 23:30–35

The goal of YHWH's ruthless techniques to clear the Land is to enable the Israelites to 'possess the Land' exclusively—the First Nations peoples of Canaan have been dispossessed and destroyed: they can no longer claim ownership of the Land.

The Israelites' incontrovertible possession of the land is the result of the intervention of YHWH. The relentless colonising of Canaan is the work of the colonial God, YHWH. The step-by-step process is outlined in explicit detail.

> Little by little I will drive them out before you
> until you are increased and
> **possess the Land.**
> I will set your boundaries from the Red Sea
> to the Sea of the Philistines
> and from the wilderness to the Euphrates.
> For **I will deliver the**
> **inhabitants of the Land into your hand**
> and you will drive them out before you.
>
> **You shall not make a covenant with them**
> or with their gods.
> They shall not dwell in your Land
> lest they make you sin against me.
> For if you serve their gods
> it will surely be a snare to you.

The boundaries suggested for this colony probably reflect the ideal Land promised in Genesis 15 to Abraham and his descendants, a Land extending from 'the river of Egypt to the great river, the River Euphrates' (Gen 15:18).

The Land initially promised in a covenant with Abraham in the Book of Genesis has been added by the colonial narrator as YHWH's promise to the people of Israel at Sinai. In the colonial tradition in Exodus, the Land to be conquered and possessed is a Promised Empire rather than a Promised Land.

The total removal of all peoples of the Land is not only designed to provide the Israelites with exclusive ownership of their Land, but also to prevent the Israelites being influenced by other peoples in the Land who worshipped other gods. If that happened, the total domination of YHWH could be at stake. The Israelites, unlike Abraham who worshipped the Canaanite God *El*, must worship only YHWH or risk losing their Land.

In this, the final stage of the revelation process, the colonial role and character of YHWH is quite explicit.

Do we, as readers of the Bible, need say thanks to the colonial narrator for taking the progressive steps necessary to introduce the famous colonial God named YHWH?

Repeating the Colonial Intentions Exodus 32–34

The remaining chapters of Exodus (32–43), which primarily deal with the ordinances specifying how Israel is to worship YHWH, include a cluster of narratives highlighting again the bold intentions of YHWH to enable the Israelites to colonise Canaan by driving out the existing inhabitants of the Land.

The first passage follows the famous molten calf legend in Exodus 32. Though YHWH is angry and ready to consume the calf worshippers, Moses dares to call on YHWH to repent of this evil plan and remember God's sworn promise to Abraham.

> Remember Abraham, Isaac and Jacob
> to whom you did swear by your self
> and to whom you said,
> I will multiply your descendants
> as the stars of heaven.

> All this Land I have promised
> I will give to your descendants
> and **they shall inherit it forever** (32:13–14).

Even though YHWH sends a plague to punish the people, he then commissions Moses to depart for the Promised Land in accordance with the oath God once made to Abraham, Isaac and Jacob. YHWH reiterates that oath in direct colonial terms, promising to send an angel before them and will personally drive out the First Nations peoples in the Land.

> To your descendants
> **I will give the land.**
> I will send an angel before you
> and I will drive out the Canaanites,
> the Amorites, the Hittites, the Perizzites,
> the Hivites and the Jebusites (33:1–2).

Even though YHWH has called the Israelites a stiff-necked people, if they obey the commands of the covenant, YHWH makes promises, and adds warnings for disobeying these commands.

> Behold, I will drive out before you
> the Amorites, the Canaanites,
> the Hittites, the Perizzites,
> the Hivites and the Jebusites.
> Take heed lest you make a covenant
> with the inhabitants of the Land,
> lest it become a snare in the midst of you.
> You shall worship no other God,
> for **YHWH, whose name is Jealous,**
> is a jealous God (34:1–14).

The danger the Israelites would face in the land of Canaan is not only that they would be seduced by so-called false gods like *Baal*, but that they might also dare, like Abraham, to make a covenant with any of the First Nations inhabitants of the Land with severe implicit consequences.

The character of YHWH as a colonial conqueror is complemented by the claim to be jealous—a God who tolerates no other gods or covenant relations with non-Israelite people, even if they are the First Nations peoples of the Land.

The colonial character of YHWH is also evident in the Book of Deuteronomy. For example, after declaring once again that YHWH will clear away the seven First Nations peoples, Moses declares duties that follow from their covenant allegiance to YHWH.

> When YHWH your God
> gives them over to you
> and you defeat them,
> then **you must utterly destroy them.**
> You must make no covenant with them
> and show them no mercy.

The colonial God YHWH is a relentless and ruthless God who is willing to do anything to create a depopulated colony for the covenant people, Israel.

Part One: Conclusion

A decolonising hermeneutic has enabled us to discern eight stages in the narrator's revelation of the name, role and character of YHWH, the ancient colonial God of Israel.

In the first stage, the name of the God involved is not specified. The God remains anonymous, either because the narrator is yet ready to reveal the name of the God who plans to deliver the Israelites from slavery or because he does not wish to reveal the actual name of the God that the midwives feared. The Israelites may still have been worshipping *El*, the God whom Abraham worshipped in Canaan.

There are other narratives in the Hebrew Scriptures where the name of the God involved is not specified. In the precolonial narrative of Genesis 1:1–25, for example, the Creator 'Spirit' hovers over the primordial waters, but the name of the Creator Spirit is not given. Significantly, First Nations people resonate with this text in Genesis and can identify the Creator Spirit of the midwives with one of the names of the Creator Spirit that First Nations Australia celebrate.

In the second stage, God speaks to Moses from the flames of the burning bush. This God does not reveal a name to Moses, but claims to be none other than the God of Abraham, Isaac and Jacob—even though the colonial narrator of the Book of Exodus informs us that the God behind the anonymous voice is named YHWH.

Throughout Exodus and other biblical books like Deuteronomy and Joshua, YHWH is disclosed to be the God of Abraham, Isaac and Jacob, the ancestors of the Israelites in Canaan, even though YHWH's name is only revealed in stage three of the colonial narrator's sequence of events in Exodus. According to this narrator, the people of Israel's association with the patriarchs is linked with the promise that their descendants would one day possess the Land of Canaan and remove its First Nations inhabitants and their claims to ownership of the Land.

Stage three is unique in respect to the name of the God in the narrative. Moses pleads his ignorance about the name of the God who is confronting him. The voice from the flames identifies the God involved as YHWH.

Nowhere else does the Hebrew Bible record an account of the Israelite God YHWH revealing a personal name. In Exodus, this event is recorded as a unique moment of Israelite history.

Earlier references to patriarchs worshipping YHWH are clearly anachronistic—especially the assertion in Genesis 4:26 where the editor claims that the family of Adam 'called on the *Name* of YHWH'.

Stage four is also surprising. Even though this God YHWH claims to be the God of Abraham, Isaac and Jacob of stage two of the narrative, the narrator only reveals the name of God known to the patriarchs in stage four—and that name, surprisingly, is the name of the Canaanite God *El Shaddai*.

Stage five is well-known in the Judeo-Christian tradition. YHWH is the God remembered for intervening in nature to enable the Israelites to escape from Egypt and cross the Reed Sea. The role of YHWH in the overpowering of the forces of nature, however, is less common in the biblical tradition, even though Joshua can evoke the power of YHWH to cause the sun to stand still.

Stage six introduces the famous Old Covenant with Israel, based on the choice of Israel as YHWH's personal people from among all the peoples of the Earth.

This covenant is renewed formally by Joshua when the Israelites have colonised Canaan after YHWH has given them the Land by sending hornets ahead of them. In Joshua 24, YHWH is identified as a jealous God who will not tolerate rival deities.

Stage seven is spectacular. YHWH appears visibly as an overwhelming fire-cloud (*kabod*) on top of Mt Sinai and invites Moses to be a mediator for the people of Israel.

In the years that follow, this fire-cloud resides in the tabernacle and then in the temple of Solomon, departing when Jerusalem is about to be conquered by foreign invaders. Interestingly, Isaiah hears the seraphim declare that 'the whole Earth/Land is full of his *kabod*' (Isa. 6.3).

Stage eight is a climax. YHWH not only promises to enable the Israelites to colonise Canaan, but also announces a frightening capacity to terrify and 'blot out' the First Nations inhabitants of Canaan.

This ruthless dimension of the character of YHWH is evident especially in Joshua. When the city of Jericho is totally destroyed, its contents—including the First Nations men, women and children—are all 'devoted to YHWH for destruction'.[1] The First Nations people of Jericho are tantamount to an unholy sacrifice to YHWH (Jos 6:16–17).

Just as there are clear stages involved in revealing the name, role and character of the colonial God YHWH in Exodus, there are several stages recalling the relationship of the people of Israel and the Land of Canaan: from settlement in a future land of milk and honey to the annihilation of all Canaanites so that Israel could 'possess' the Land as their own colony with no competing claims to First Nations ownership.

- Recalling God's link with the fathers, this God promises to bring the Israelites to the Land of the Canaanites, a Land flowing with milk and honey (3:17)
- Recalling God's covenant with the fathers, God promises to give them the Land of Canaan, the Land in which they were initially sojourners (6:4)
- The Israelites are expected to celebrate the 'Passover' in the Land that YHWH will give them (12:15)
- The outcome of the commandment to 'honour father and mother' means the Israelites will live long on the Land YHWH gives them (20:12)
- To colonise the Land of Canaan, the First Nations peoples— Amorites, Canaanites, Hittites, Perizzites, Hivites, Jebusites— must eventually be 'blotted out' since the Israelites might be seduced by the gods of Canaan (23:23–24)

---

1. This technical term is tantamount to a bloody sacrifice. The sacrifice in Jos 6:1 is a *cherem*, an unholy sacrifice or slaughter dedicated to YHWH.

- The process of colonisation by 'blotting out' the Canaanites will be the result of YHWH sending 'terror' to overwhelm the Canaanites (23:26)
- This process will enable the Israelites to 'possess' their own Land as a colony (23.10).

Just as there is a clear and widely celebrated progression in the narrative plot from slavery in Egypt to a covenant at Mt Sinai, there is also a progression in the relationship of the Israelites and the promised Land of Canaan, a relationship from a Land flowing with milk and honey to a land full of First Nations peoples perceived as pagans who must be blotted out so that YHWH may forever be Israel's only God.

This study has highlighted how in the Book of Exodus, the colonialist narrator revealed YHWH not only as the jealous God of ancient Israel, but also as the colonial God who is intent on destroying all the First Nations peoples of Canaan so that this God's chosen people can colonise the Land forever.

PART TWO
The Challenge and Responses

The name of the colonial God, YHWH, persists throughout the Hebrew Scriptures, even though the name is translated 'Lord'.

The challenge we face is to discover how and where biblical narrators—prophets, priests, wise—modify the role and character of YHWH so that the overt colonial features outlined above are modified—or even deleted—and the portrayal of YHWH in the narrative is different.

We can use the opening verses of Psalm 23 in the Book of Psalms, to demonstrate how the text can be read differently. 'YHWH is my shepherd I shall now want. He makes my lie down in green pastures.'

Moses, with his experience and the understanding of YHWH revealed in Exodus, might perceive this text in the following ways.

- YHWH is my warrior God
  I need not surrender
  He 'blots out' all my enemies.

or

- YHWH is my jealous God,
  I dare not disobey.

We face the same challenge when we read the Christian Scriptures. Is the God of Jesus and the narrators of the Gospels related to the colonial God of the Hebrew Scriptures, or radically different? The name YHWH does not appear in the Greek text of the *Septuagint*.[1]

---

1. As we are focussing on the Bible text accepted by most Christians, we do not refer to these other versions, often referred to as the 'Dead Sea Scrolls'—discovered in the twentieth century in caves near the Dead Sea..

Jesus' Sermon on the Mount may be compared to Moses' commandments from Mount Sinai. Jesus may have said that he came to fulfil the law and the prophets (Mat. 5.17), but he interprets the will of the Father quite differently in the famous text attributed to him in Matthew 5.44.[2]

> Love your enemies
> and pray for those
> who persecute you
> so that you may be sons
> of your Father in heaven.

We face a further challenge when we wonder about the God of the European missionaries and early Christian teachers. They would have baptised in the 'name of the Father, the Son and the Holy Spirit'.

Did they explore the role and character of the 'Lord God' of Sinai and the Exodus?

Even more poignant, were early European missionaries familiar with—or even supported—the popular claim that the God who promised the Land of Canaan to the Israelites provided a precedent for European settlers to colonise the 'Promised Land' of Australia? Is there any hint that missionaries, familiar with the Bible, were aware of the colonial character of YHWH in the Book of Exodus?

In 1992, when the citizens of the Barossa erected a monument to celebrate 150 years in their 'Promised Land', they quoted Joshua 2.9 on the monument using the following words: 'The Lord has given us this Land!'

They may have been unaware that 'the Lord' was indeed YHWH, but they still believed that the promise of God to Joshua was valid for Barossa Lutherans.

Vicky Balabanski Response

We asked Vicky Balabanski to share her responses to the argument presented in this book.

---

2. Most scholars agree that we do not have a book written by Jesus himself. The gospels present different perspectives of Jesus, narrated from oral recollections of those who lived at the time of Jesus.

(The 1992 Barossa Monument)

Vicky is a New Testament scholar who has been working with Anne Pattel-Gray and Uncle Norm in developing and applying a decolonising hermeneutic in our reading of the Genesis texts. She has also become 'colonial conscious' in her work with First Nations Australia.

This is her response.

Eugene Petersen once wrote that we 'don't become more spiritual by becoming less human.'[3]

Uncle Norm is giving us a way to see the process whereby the most ancient revelation of God—the Creator Spirit deeply connected with the Land and all its creatures—is adapted to a different narrative perspective, one where power and might are right.

To perceive this shift embedded in the biblical narrative—a shift from precolonial to procolonial—is disturbing and important.

---

3. Eugene Peterson *The Word Made Flesh: The Language of Jesus in His Stories and Prayers* (London: Hodder & Stoughton, 2008), chapter.3.

Biblical scholars have long known that there are strands and perspectives in the Pentateuch, the first five books of the Bible. But no one to date has proposed quite the sort of 'stratigraphy' that Uncle Norm is putting forward, based on the way the YHWH traditions have not only shifted away from the earlier El traditions, but have also shifted from liberation of an oppressed people towards colonial conquest and genocide.

In the Bible we do not have a simply unified rule book. We have a complex library, edited to reflect later contexts and times and values. First Nations peoples are invited by Uncle Norm to see a different perspective—one that is closer to *El Elyon, El Shaddai* and *El Olam*, the names of the Indigenous god of the Canaanites.

This is the god of the priest of Salem, who welcomed Abraham when he defended the local people of Canaan (Gen 14). Abraham made a treaty with the Indigenous peoples of Canaan and affirmed their faith in *El*, the Creator Spirit of the Land of Canaan.

Why was this tradition overlooked by the missionaries?

For us, it is challenging to recognise that the Exodus stories— so important in providing a narrative of liberation for oppressed peoples—in the hands of settlers and colonial powers are themselves a source of oppression. We cannot see everything that YHWH is recorded to have done as tainted, yet when the oppressed becomes the oppressor, we must object.

Authors Response

The response of Vicky Balabanski highlights how an ancient understanding of God can be adapted where power and might are believed to be right. This adaptation is summarised by Vicky as the shift from '*pre*colonial to *pro*colonial', a shift that Vicky rightly identifies as 'disturbing and important' especially in the light of the compassionate God proclaimed by Jesus of Nazareth.

To recognise the shift from *El*, the Creator Spirit of the Land, to YHWH, the colonial God of Israel, is also disturbing for First Nations Australia. That shift is a parallel painful reality that they have experienced as a result of colonisation too.

Vicky also poses the crucial question of why the tradition of the Creator Spirit in Canaan was overlooked by missionaries. The compassionate God that Abraham knew is very different from the violent colonial God Moses knew. I have explored this question in my volume entitled, *Acknowledgement of the Land and Faith of Aboriginal Custodians after Following the Abraham Trail.*[4]

Another factor is the realisation that by focusing on the Exodus tradition as the liberation of the oppressed Israelites in Egypt, we have ignored how the colonial God YHWH enabled the oppressed people of Israel to become the colonial oppressors of the Canaanites with whom Abraham had made a treaty in the name of their God, *El.*

Thanks, Vicky, for acknowledging that the liberation of the oppressed Israelites in Egypt is in no way a narrative for First Nations Australia peoples to find liberation. The exodus from Egypt was a major step in the process of colonisation promised by the colonial God, YHWH.

Robert Kempe Response

We invited Robert Kempe, whose grandfather was a missionary at Hermannsburg in Central Australia, whether the diaries of his grandfather provide answers to the challenges above. This is his response.

During the last four years I have been working with a colleague to translate from German into English all the available reports of the first Hermannsburg-on-the-Finke mission staff.[5] Altogether there are over 400 reports, most of them were written by the first three missionaries to the Finke: AH Kempe (my great-grandfather) and WF Schwarz— first to arrive in Australia in 1875—and LG Schulze who arrived a couple of years later. A fourth major contributor to these reports was the Superintendent of the Mission: GA Heidenreich, the Lutheran pastor in Bethany.

One of the fascinating aspects of engaging in this translation work is how it has taken me into the minds and thinking of these men. Yet, despite what I have learnt about them, it is not easy to provide a clear and concise response to the challenges Norm issues in relation to YHWH, the colonial God.

Like many other missions, the Finke mission did invade and take over Aboriginal Land—Kempe actually uses the word 'invade' in at least one of his reports. The missionaries also refer to the lay-helpers who came with them as 'colonists/settlers'.

---

4. Habel, *Acknowledgement*, 2018.
5. These reports were written between 1875 and 1892; the mission was located in South Australia.

Together they occupied something like 2500 square kilometres of Land around Hermannsburg. They brought sheep, cattle, horses and bullocks into this land, and they worked the land, built on the land and, yes, destroyed much of the natural flora and fauna and waterholes of the Land in the process. In this sense I guess they 'colonised' it. They also certainly colonised the Land in the sense that they desired to impose Western culture and moral values upon the lives of the *Aranda* people.[6]

Thus, if YHWH is the God who colonises, and if the missionaries came—as they claim—to do God's work, then it would seem logical to conclude that these missionaries and colonists were acting as servants of YHWH, the colonial God.

However, I do not believe they consciously thought that way—at least not in Hermannsburg.

In fact, I think these particular missionaries would have been pretty flummoxed by any suggestion that—as for Israel, so for them— YHWH had given them some divine right to this Land, and that they were called to rid the Land of its inhabitants and establish some kind of new nation of their own making.

The reason these particular missionaries went to Hermannsburg— and I assume this is true of many other missionaries in Australia— was their deep and sincere concern for the spiritual wellbeing of the Aboriginal peoples.

That concern may have been naïve and prejudiced, and it may often have been ignorant of and insensitive to any notion of God the Aboriginal peoples living in this Land already had.

Nevertheless, it was a genuine concern grounded in a notion of God more akin to *El Shaddai*, the Creator Spirit God who desires the wellbeing of his creation (as outlined in stage four).

But for these missionaries that understanding of God was steeped in their Lutheran theology, which grounded them in a view of humanity that deems all non-Christian people—Aboriginal or not— as naturally alienated from God and incapable of doing anything to reverse that condition. Thus the missionaries consistently refer to the Aboriginal peoples as 'heathen' and 'a deeply-sunken people'.

Despite that, their God is a God of love and grace who desires the redemption of all people—a redemption freely offered and made real through the vicarious death of Jesus Christ and imparted to human

---

6. The name of the First Nations Australia people living on the Land.

beings through Word and Sacrament. This is the God the missionaries desired to make known to the Aboriginal peoples, and whom they proclaimed. And that God is not YHWH, the colonial God.

But there are two other factors that confuse that claim.

First of all, there is the fact that the mission did 'take over' the Land.

However, they did this not as a means of dispersing and displacing the Aboriginal peoples, but rather as a means of having a place with the Aboriginal peoples where they engaged together in the work of mission. This was an important part of the explicit mission vision of Hermannsburg, the mission station where the Aboriginal peoples could live and work and eat in safety, and where they could grow together as a Christian community.

Far from taking the Land away from those First Nations peoples, the missionaries desired to work alongside them in keeping and developing their Land. And when, later, pastoralists and others sought to disperse and even eradicate the Aboriginal peoples from their Land, the mission became a sanctuary and advocate for an endangered people—quite the opposite of what the God YHWH might do!

And the second confusing factor in the way the missionaries related God to the lives of the Aboriginal peoples had to do with what happened after these First Nations peoples became Christian.

Here, sadly, they were confronted with the Colonial Covenant (as described in stage 6) of the God YHWH. The covenant demanded an expectation of obedience to 'law'. Once they became Christian, the First Nations Australia peoples were expected to live as Christians; there were severe punishments, including chains and whippings, for those who disobeyed.

John Harris addresses this problem in his book, *One Blood*,[7] although he has not quite got hold of the Lutheran nuances in this complicated matter.

> It is hardly surprising that the Aranda rejected this unbalanced version of the gospel; hardly surprising that they rejected a 'good news' that was barely good news at all; hardly surprising they found unacceptable the teaching that in order to find

---

7. John Harris, *One Blood. 2000 years of Aboriginal Encounter with Christianity. A Story of Hope* (Sutherland: Albatross, 1990), 394.

acceptance with God through Jesus Christ, they had first to give up everything they had known, all that they had ever been, regard it as evil and adopt alien, European patterns of life.

What the missionaries expected of the baptised Aboriginal people was not as blanket as that. But, in essence, Harris' observation is valid.

One could well ask what 'law' it was that the missionaries believed the Aranda should understand . . . It was almost certainly not the Mosaic Law, but the Lutheran's own strict and legalised version of Christian behaviour.[8]

Again, as it stands, that statement is partly true and but needs some nuancing within the Lutheran understanding of justification and sanctification and the various uses of the Law. Harris concludes—and I resonate with his conclusion.

It is sad that the missionaries were not prepared simply to share their knowledge of Christ with the Aranda and allow them to determine the extent to which Christ's teachings might challenge the negative or undesirable features of their own culture. They failed to realise that the Aranda lived a life of obedience to law far more truly and deeply than the missionaries could begin to understand.[9]

In the final analysis, it is vital to remember that, in seeking to resolve the varying and sometimes conflicting themes of the Norm challenge, we are working within three different worldviews.

- The worldview of the First Nations Australia and their spiritualty and culture.
- The worldview of the missionaries, shaped by their theology and culture.
- Our worldview today, shaped especially by its pluralism and multi-culturalism.

We each are people of our own time, place and history; and, for me, it is important to listen to each other across the centuries, to seek to understand each other—even if we disagree—and to respect each other.

That, in my opinion, is the authentic pathway to any needed reconciliation.

---

8. Harris, *One Blood*, 395.
9. Harris, *One Blood*, 396.

Authors Response

The response of Robert Kempe highlights the historical reality that we and our ancestors have lived in a range of diverse cultures, each of which has a distinctive worldview. Robert identifies these cultures as

> culture of First Nations Australia and the profound spiritual worldview they knew and celebrated, a worldview that most missionaries dismissed
>
> the culture of the German missionaries whose worldview was influenced by their Lutheran theology and a mission to 'Christianise Aborigines'
>
> The culture of those early settlers/colonists whose worldview accepted the process of colonisation as valid or, in some cases, as divinely approved
>
> the culture of contemporary Australian society that is generally shaped by pluralism, multiculturalism and a scientific worldview.

To extend the debate further, we need to be aware that the peoples who lived in these cultures accepted their culture as definitive for their faith or consciousness. Rarely did they readily enter into dialogue with the peoples of another culture.

If we take a step further back into history, we begin to realise that there were radically different cultures and worldviews throughout history that are relevant for our discussion:

- the culture of the ancient Canaanites whose worldview the Abraham community accepted and celebrated
- the culture of the narrator of the Book of Exodus whose worldview involved reading and affirming the role and character of YHWH as the colonial God who justified the destruction of the Canaanites and who introduced a rigorous colonial covenant for his chosen people
- the culture of the Israelites who returned from exile in Babylon, where they preserved their diverse cultural traditions in the Hebrew Scriptures and anticipated a new age of hope in the so-called 'Promised Land'
- the culture of the pious Jewish community under Roman rule who anticipated liberation from alien influence.

- the radical culture Jesus announced involving a worldview entitled 'the Kingdom of God' in which 'love' was the force that would govern all relationships; he was even reported to have said, 'Love your enemies!'

While missionaries may have sought to incorporate the culture espoused by Jesus and his followers, their missiology and European worldview would have meant they belonged to a very different culture to that of Jesus.

Given these factors, it is understandable that despite the colonial worldview of the early settlers and missionaries, their culture was radically different from the culture associated with the colonial God YHWH reflected in the books of Exodus and Joshua.

The colonial culture associated with the original God YHWH may lie in the background.

However, we believe it is important to become aware of this background, to expose the colonial YHWH culture as irrelevant in contemporary Australia, and that it is vitally important that we decolonise our thinking in future dialogues with First Nations Australia.

In the current Australian context, is the colonial God YHWH tantamount to an outdated God or even a false God?

As Robert Crotty has stated, reconciliation demands we acknowledge the spiritual culture of First Nations Australia.

And we would add that we need to acknowledge that the long history of colonial cultures has conditioned us to possess a latent colonial consciousness. We believe we need to dismiss the colonial God YHWH as an outdated part of our heritage and to intensify our dialogue with First Nations Australia about the relevance for contemporary Australian Christians and for all Australian Christians of the Creator Spirit they have experienced here in this Land.

Jione Havea Response

We also invited Jione Havea to respond to the challenge posed by this analysis of Exodus.

He is not only a scholar familiar with interpretation of the biblical text, but also a First Nations pastor who is acutely aware of the role of Christian missions in the colonisation of the Pacific Islands of Oceania, and the ability of 'noble empires' of the modern time to disguise perpetual colonial projects.

Talanoa with/around Norm's challenge

I am grateful to Authors for this opportunity to engage with his reading of the Exodus narrative, and i[10] present my Response in the spirit of *talanoa*.

The term '*talanoa*' is used in several of the Pasifika languages for three interlinked events:

- story—usually includes several stories
- telling stories
- conversation or story-weaving.

The term *talanoa* refers to all three: story, telling, conversation. A story (*talanoa*) is dead without someone to tell (*talanoa*) it and listeners to engage with both the story and its telling in conversation (*talanoa*); a telling (*talanoa*) becomes a 'telling off' or 'lecture' if there is no story (*talanoa*) as content and no conversation (*talanoa*) as response; and a conversation (*talanoa*) requires both story (*talanoa*) and telling (*talanoa*).

A *talanoa* is a native event that shapes my mind and work. I make this connection: Authors has presented his *talanoa* (interlinking stories) and invited me to join his *talanoa* event. I do so as a native pastor, from the islands of Tonga.

The natives of the sea of islands in Oceania lived with, and under the influence of, the spirits and energies of the sea, the land, the underworld, and the skies—before the *pālangi* (white, European) traders, missionaries, and colonisers arrived.

There were native names for those spirits and energies including *atua* (Tuvalu, Māori, Samoa), *akua* (Hawai'i), *'otua* (Tonga), *'oro* (Ma'ohinui), *kalou* (Fiji). There were MANY names—even before considering the more than one thusand native languages in Papua, Solomon, and Vanuatu.

When the *pālangi* arrived, they brought their ideas of 'god'. They hijacked the native names and used those for their (foreign) gods. In contexts where there were multiple names to choose between, the *pālangi* chose one—for example, in translations of the Bible .

On this front, two crimes were committed.

---

10. Jione Havea requested that a lower case 'I' be used as the first person singular pronoun in his response.

- First, the hijack of native names as if *atua*, for example, referred to the same spirits and energies for the natives as 'god' did for the *pālangi*; this was not translation but a hijack of the native names as well as of the respect that natives held for the spirits and energies of the sea, the Land, the underworld, and the skies. In hijacking native terms, the *pālangi* also colonised native languages especially through bible translation projects. The colonising of native languages resulted in the colonising of native minds, native souls, native faiths, and everything else that shaped what it means to be native.
- Second, the reduction of the pantheon of spirits and energies for natives—*atua* was the generic name for *Tangaroa, Papatūānuku, Haumiatiketike, Rongomātāne,* and many other native peoples' gods—to 'god' as a singular being as imagined by *pālangi* was part of their colonising, monotheistic agenda.

The colonial project involved discounting rival spirits and energies. Coloniality, like Christianity, hid the inability to cope with 'many-ness' under the mask of 'unification'.

From the context of Oceania, therefore, Norm's reading of the Exodus narrative makes a lot of sense: YHWH is a colonial god revealed in stages in the Exodus narrative, and the Exodus narrators **suppressed** the names, the roles, and the divinities of the spirits and energies— gods—of the Canaanites and put them under the feet of YHWH.

And, lest we forget, the people of Israel—devotees of YHWH in the book of Exodus—are a colonial people.

Before contact with the *pālangi*, the natives of Oceania were familiar with *atua*—in my following comments, i'll use this native name for god to represent the spirits and energies of the Land, the sea, the underworld, and the skies scuffling with one another.

In Aotearoa, for instance, *Ranginui*—the sky *atua*—and *Papatūānuku* —the earth *atua*—were joined and their children were born in the darkness between them. Their children decided to separate them, so that there will be light on earth and so that they could play and live apart from their parents. The children pushed their parents apart and they consequently became *atua* in different areas: *Tagaroa* in the sea, *Tāne* in the forest.

A longer reflection by Tangata Whenua—indigenous person of Aotearoa—unpacks this Māori creation narrative, but my drive here is to show that

1. having many *atua* was not a problem for the natives of Oceania
2. scuffling between the many *atua* was part of the native story-worlds. In this connection, i don't find the scuffles between YHWH and the various local names of *El*, the god of Canaan, strange.

What i find problematic is that the colonial process of 'one-ification'—reducing the many to 'one'—gives supremacy to YHWH. For, in the Māori story world, *Ranginui* and *Papatūānuku* were separated and their children became *atua* for the many regions of life. There is no supreme *atua*; the separation between *Ranginui* and *Papatūānuku* resulted in more *atua*, who collaborated in keeping life ticking until the next scuffle. And the next recuperation. And so on.

As a native, i welcome Norm's reading and challenge. And i natively invite further *talanoa* around two other native subjects in the Exodus narrative.

First, the normal people of Egypt. They are presented as citizens of an empire, and they are silently condemned, both in the narrative and in readings of the narrative, because of the wickedness of their Pharaoh, a generic name for god/*atua*. Put another way, the normal native people of Egypt are thrown under the bus because of their god, Pharaoh. The power of the narrative to justify the squashing of Pharaoh and Egypt also blinds readers from seeing the disguised injustice against the normal people of Egypt.

Second, the native people of the wilderness. The imperial YHWH, and his colonising people, did not start their colonising project when they arrived at Canaan. Colonisation started even in the wilderness. The colonising people of YHWH were trespassing through the homes of the people in the wilderness: the Midianites, the Amalekites, and many other peoples on their way to Canaan. Put directly, the wilderness was not empty Land.

What does reading YHWH, as colonial god, say and do for the normal peoples of Egypt, and for the native peoples in the wilderness?

Authors Response

The response of Jione Havea highlights not only the plight of the Israelites at the hand of the Pharaoh of Egypt, but also the unjust suffering of the peoples of Egypt because of Pharaoh's actions and attitude. Ultimately, we can also acknowledge that the misery and pain of the ordinary Egyptian people is the result of the cruel disasters initiated by the colonial God YHWH; YHWH punishes all Egyptians for the sins of Pharaoh.

In another context[11] We have discussed not only how the people of Egypt suffered without justification, but also that the natural realms of the Nile, the Land and the living creatures were the object of devastating misery at the hand of the colonial God YHWH. YHWH's colonial cruelty in Egypt preceded terrifying acts of violence in the Land of Canaan.[12]

As Jione indicated, similar colonial deeds persisted in the wilderness where the Israelites dispossessed Amorites (Num. 21.22) and other tribes living in the wilderness. The colonial character of YHWH persisted even in the wilderness.

Jione Havea also raises another issue about the revelation of YHWH as the God of Israel that is rarely explored—namely, the origin of monolatry. Jione observes that 'i find problematic . . . that the colonial process of 'one-ification'—reducing the many to 'one'—gives supremacy to YHWH'.

One may wish to read the claim that YHWH was one and the same God as *El*, the Canaanite Creator Spirit, as a clue that the God-world of Canaan has been assumed under one head, the God YHWH. The result of this 'one-ification' is that no other God of Egypt, the wilderness or Canaan is to be tolerated because YHWH is a jealous God and claims control of all domains of the universe, whether physical or spiritual.

The option of discerning diverse spiritual forces in the world, a reality experienced by First Nations Australia, is dismissed as being intolerable by the jealous God YHWH.

Many thanks Jione for your insights and affirmation.

---

11. Habel, *An Inconvenient Truth*.
12. Habel, *An Inconvenient Truth*, 16–19.

Anne Pattel-Gray Response

Anne Pattel-Gray has been a pivotal person in the origin of the decolonising hermeneutic that we have developed in this series entitled Decolonising the Biblical Narrative.

Her response arises not only from her profound knowledge of the biblical narrative, but also from her personal experience, and that of her First Nations ancestors, of the colonial curse in Australia.

Colonial Bondage: Liberating Biblical Narratives

In 2016 I had the opportunity to meet Professor Norm Habel at the national Common Dreams conference held in Sydney, Australia and there we discussed our biblical and theological views. During this conversation I asked Norm if he was open to working with me to decolonise biblical narratives beginning with Genesis; his response was yes. So began our exploration with the development of our hermeneutical process that we would take to decolonise Genesis.

I wish to take this opportunity to express my deepest gratitude to Norm as I acknowledge his courage in giving me insights into the Hebrew narratives of Genesis and to open wide this world to me, a non-biblical scholar.

Norm's incredible willingness to deconstruct and to decolonise these biblical narratives has exposed the colonial bondage that has encapsulated the colonisers' interpretation of biblical narratives to legitimate their colonisation of Australia.

Australia's First Nations people's faith has been nurtured over thousands of years and as a result we have a very intimate relationship with the Creator Spirit. When we speak of this relationship, we invoke the Spirit Creator in our midst. Our Ancestral Narratives reflect this relationship, and our ceremonies give praise to our Creator and remind us of our obligations to one another, to Land, environment and the whole of creation, to our Law and the responsibilities given to us by the Creator Spirit. Among Australia's First Nations peoples there are power-filled stories about the Creator Spirit's acts in the very beginning—we are considered the oldest living culture in the world.

Australia's First Nations Christian leaders say their Ancestral Narratives speak about our knowledge of, and belief in, a Creator Spirit who, through our Spirit Ancestors, formed our world and forged our identity, culture and law. This process highlights the relationship of Australia's First Nations peoples to the Land, creation, the environment and the spiritual world of our Spirit Ancestors and the Creator Spirit, and how they are all linked to each other and dependent upon this interconnection. Our Faith and the spiritual world were—and still are—the life-force and foundation of our life, existence and survival. The Creator Spirit is the source of life for us, and, as our Spiritual leaders state, we cannot survive without our connection to this life source.

First Nations Australia peoples have a deep understanding of the divinity associated with the Creator Spirit as this has been nurtured over some 110,000 years.

The Creator Spirit is the creator of our world, and the creator of our humanity. We are born in the image of the Creator Spirit, and we are who we are because of the Creator Spirit. We have an intuitive sense of God as Creator Spirit, as a wisdom teacher on country, and as Spirit.

The Creator Spirit bestowed upon us our Land and entrusted this world to us, and we are to protect, care for and to rejuvenate our Earth Mother.

The Creator Spirit handed down our Law that dictates every aspect of our life and permeates our spiritual life and teaches us how to care for our country and our obligations and responsibilities to our kinship system, religious and spiritual life. The Creator Spirit gave us our ceremonies, songs and rituals that honour—and remind us—of the Creator's presence and that the Creator is always with us.

Western Colonial Domination

In 1788 the British invaded our Lands and so began the forced indoctrination of Australian Christendom that would be the beginning of our nightmare.

The colonisers dominated every aspect of the Bible from biblical interpretation to the point where the text was used to justify colonial theft and dispossession, subjugation and oppression, massacres and cultural genocide, and the rape of women and children. This also formed the basis on which we were cursed, deemed demonic and a racially inferior race of people.

The colonial invaders with their racist views believed their 'whiteness' made them superior[13] and they considered Australia's

---

13. Pattel-Gray, *The Great White Flood.*.

First Nation Australia peoples as being inferior and morally bankrupt. What the colonisers failed to see was the rich spiritual life of Aboriginal people and the presence of Creator Spirit in us.

These days, Australia's First Nations peoples continue to experience racial discrimination when the Federal government suspends the Racial Discrimination Act that protects the Human Rights of Australia's First Nations people; this enables the continuing removal of our children from their families and communities, and allows governments to take control our peoples incomes, and results in the high incarceration rates of First Nations children and young people, high suicide rates of our young people and the denial of cultural rights and heritage. In addition, successive governments have failed to formalise a treaty with Australia's First Nations peoples.

The horrific acts that have been inflicted upon Australia's First Nations peoples have had a deep psychological impact on the lives of my people that has left them traumatised—and the effect of this trauma is still being felt today.

Sadly, the most frightening aspect of the Christian church's complicity in the subjugation of First Nations peoples is the heartfelt sentiment usually expressed that it was done 'with the best of intentions'.

This, however, does not alleviate the enormous trauma inflicted upon my people. The forced imposition of the Christian missionaries and, in fact, those churches that worked among Australia's First Nations communities, were partners with the government in the genocide.

Unwittingly no doubt, and always 'with the best of intentions'; nevertheless, the missionaries and churches were guilty of complicity in the destruction of First Nations cultures and tribal social structures and complicit in the devastating impoverishment and death of the people to whom they preached.

Other genocidal acts led to the crushing of Australia's First Nations people's identity and religious and spiritual beliefs. The history of colonisation can be seen as the domination of the Western world. Whether this is good or bad thing, it has impacted the psychical, emotional and psychological lives of First Nations people resulting in intergenerational trauma through the vehicle of missionisation—this methodological process, leading to the historical experiences and current experiences of continuing racism, discrimination and marginalisation—is still our lived reality.

The legacy of 'colonial Christianity'[14] and its effects on both First Nations and colonial participants in the missionisation process means there is a critical need to identify and to reaffirm our Aboriginal spirituality and cultural heritage as the first step in our struggle for religious self-determination. The recognition of this need began the search for a process to decolonise our theology and to remove all its Western bias.

Colonial Narratives

As a First Nations theologian from Australia, I have always struggled with the colonial narrative that portrays a Colonial God, YHWH, who favours one race over another—this tradition has been used to justify Western colonisers who identify themselves as the 'Chosen Ones'. I cannot believe that this colonial God is one and the same as the Creator Spirit that we know and understand, and in whose spirit we breathe.

This colonial God, YHWH, that the coloniser brought with them to our Land, was and still is hell-bent on destroying First Nations people. We can no longer tolerate bearing the image of this God; nor can we find comfort in, or communion with, a God who acted like a colonial landlord.

It is imperative that by returning to the images of Creator Spirit prevalent in our First Nations culture and spirituality, we can decolonise this colonial God; we must decolonise both biblical and theological narratives that support this colonial God YHWH.

As a First Nations people, our faith has been nurtured over thousands of years and as a result we have a very intimate relationship with the Creator Spirit. When we speak of this relationship, we invoke the Spirit Creator in our midst. Our Ancestral Narratives reflect this relationship, and our ceremonies give praise to our Creator and remind us of our obligations to one another, to the Land and the environment, to the Law and the responsibilities given to us by the Creator Spirit.

Our image of God is unlike the one portrayed by many colonial churches and missionaries, who presented God as dwelling at a

---

14. For a more comprehensive history of Australian church mission activity and its impact on the First Nations of this land, see Harris, *One Blood*.

distance, and living in heaven in splendid isolation. Many early missionaries did not discern either that God was present in the Land of Australia, or the high level of spirituality that was present in our Aboriginal culture long before they appeared.

First Nations people cannot help but contemplate that this colonial God is a distant ruler who has handed over to the human coloniser the whole created order as a resource under their oversight and for their own use and benefit. Their colonial God is a faraway king who has ceded control of all the animals and plants to human servants. This God instructs human assistants to rule over what has been entrusted to them. If God, the heavenly monarch, has handed the whole created order over to the human colonists as landlords, the outcome is that they, in turn, are free to do what they want with it.

This is further apparent in Western Christian interpretation that they are the 'Chosen Ones'. This reading paved the way for colonisers' early attacks on the First Nations people's religious and spiritual beliefs that a sacred spirit permeates all nature. This colonial concept of God as a disembodied deity uninterested in earthly affairs stripped the world of any spiritual significance or meaning. This created a separation between our kinship with our environment.

Decolonising Biblical Narratives

It is important that the churches and Christians realise how essential it is for First Nation Australia and all Christians to decolonise the biblical narratives. In order for Australia's First Nations peoples to do this, we need to

- restore our relationship first with the Creator Spirit
- make a radical transformation that sees us reconnecting physically and spiritually with the Land and our common kinship with each other and all creation
- understand our human necessity to see ourselves as part of creation but not as a power over nature
- regard ourselves as living in creation and creation as being important to our very existence
- recognise our longing for, and restore our primordial sense of belonging to Mother Earth: our existence is dependent on her.

As my people have stated over the past several decades that Adam and Eve could not have been Aboriginal because if they were, they would have eaten the snake and not the apple! Based on this understanding, Adam and Eve would not have been the basis for Original Sin entering the world.

As First Nations people, we believe sin first entered the world because of colonisation; Western colonisation and Christianity became the vehicle through which they transported through indoctrination their cultural views and baggage to make others inferior to them.

As a First Nations theologian the development of my theology could not be done without setting out the experiential context and consequences of the suffering, subjugation and oppression of my people. Experience, both historical and current, defines the First Nations peoples' anguish and their responses to the cruelty of Western colonisation and missionisation in Australia, including

- the theft of Land
- genocidal acts
- slavery
- segregation
- the government and church process of removing thousands of Aboriginal children from their mothers, referred to as the 'stolen generations'
- the Western environmental destruction of Aboriginal Land and life-ways.[15]

First Nations men, women and children possess an affinity with the Land, and, through our Spirit, we feel the heartbeat of our Mother Earth: we are inextricability bound to her for survival.

This colonial view of a God is one that separates the Creator Spirit from creation but is not one that First Nations people can relate to at all—the Creator Spirit is the centre of our universe and the life-force of our Mother Earth on which all life depends for survival. We cannot comprehend a life that is not Creator-centred.

The role of First Nations women is considered critical to the maintenance, continuity and survival of the entire societal structure. First Nations society, as we knew it then and as it still is, depends on the equal participation of women.

---

15. Pattel-Gray, *The Great White Flood*.

Today, the status and position of First Nations women within Australia differs, depending upon the impact and absorption of the colonisation, missionisation and Western patriarchal beliefs and misogynist acts in our society. Western colonial biblical interpretation and Western values have done much to undermine the status and role of First Nations women throughout our Land. That is why it is critical for biblical narratives to be decolonised in order to dismantle and hopefully eradicate colonial power and domination and these will give way to the empowerment of all First Nations people around the world.

From our perspective, this blatant colonial tradition that confirms the original harsh mandate to dominate the Land and all living creatures of the Land (Gen 1:26–28), also reflects the colonial worldview and colonial actions of the Europeans peoples who invaded and colonised the Land of Australia. Our response is to discern the falsity of this biblical tradition, recall the truths of our First Nations relationship with the Land and the Land beings of our Country and to endorse the alternate interpretation of our ancient traditions.

As First Nations theologians, we are free to take this stand because of our rich spiritual relationship with the Land and the Creator Spirit in the Land. We can also take this stand because we believe that Christ has liberated us from the sin of colonial control and freed us to correct ancient biblical narratives and retrieve the underlying spirit of the Gospel that is colonial-free.

Today, we challenge the colonial inheritors who continue to benefit from this colonial structure, laws, and systems as the descendants of the colonisers. They have inherited great power, wealth and privilege, resulting from the barbaric acts of their forefathers upon my people, including the theft of our Lands through legal fictions, massacres of literally thousands of my people, the multiple generations of stolen children, and the 235 years of oppression and subjugation.

The Australian church's racism is evident in its abysmal failure to stand united against racism in this country. Recognising the existence of racism in general is the easy part, and many churches decry this 'evil' in the widest possible terms. Some churches even go the next step and recognise the existence of racism in the church itself.

The church's silence is deafening. The church's lack of action is shocking.

By keeping quiet, the Australian churches are accepting the situation of racism against Aboriginal people, and implicitly espousing the cause of the privileged white majority. The churches are reinforcing their own racism, as well as that of society in general. They are endorsing inequality and injustice.[16]

In conclusion, I must therefore state if we are to have any hope of reconciliation and restoring wholeness in creation then we First Nations people must first begin by challenging the colonial inheritors' ways of doing theology on stolen Land, and what it means for them to be seen as colonial inheritors.

It is time for 'Truth Telling' and exposing the lies, brutality and the power, privilege and wealth colonial inheritors have gained througgh the injustices committed against First Nations people.

Norm Habel Reply

Anne's response to our analysis of the colonial God YHWH outlined in the Book of Exodus illustrates not only how colonisation has oppressed and subjugated First Nations Australia. She also demonstrates the influence that the beliefs of the colonial oppressors had on the spirituality of First Nations Australia.

She maintains that our analysis portrays how a colonial God, called YHWH, 'favours one race over another because this tradition has been used to justify Western colonisers who identify themselves as the Chosen Ones' and who believed that they were free to colonise the Land by approval of their 'colonial landlord'.

This colonial God is identified in Exodus as an overpowering celestial deity called YHWH whose character is radically different from that of the compassionate Creator Spirit of the Land who has inspired and guided the peoples of First Nations Australia.

Decolonising the biblical narrative of Exodus ultimately means that when First Nations peoples of Australia decolonise the colonial God of Exodus, they are free to celebrate the God of their First Nations tradition.

Decolonising this biblical narrative liberates First Nations Christians from the oppressive tradition of the Colonial God, YHWH.

---

16. Pattel-Gray, *The Great White Flood*, 159.

Conclusion

Uncle Norm

I have published numerous books as a so-called biblical scholar, but this volume may be a frightening finale. It is probably as radical and controversial as anything I have written.

Yet, it is a rewarding conclusion to my writings.

At the seminary I was taught that the text of the Bible was the inerrant inspired word of God sent directly from Above. Over the years I have discovered that the biblical text is the outcome of literary, historical and theological factors. I have also discovered that the narrators and editors of the text reflected the concerns and issues of their diverse religious cultures.

My final discovery has been the result of listening to First Nations Australia, whose mentors made me conscious not only of the cultural contexts of the biblical authors and editors, but also that I too was raised and educated with an Australian worldview, and with a colonial perspective as a 'white Australian'.

My First Nations mentors helped me to face the colonial curse I had hidden and, with them, to decolonise the biblical text. My conversation was more than just hermeneutical; it was also spiritual.

After working through Genesis with my First Nations tutors, I have explored the Book of Exodus with a decolonised consciousness.

What I had previously read as an exciting liberation tradition in which the God of Israel liberated the Israelites from slavery in Egypt and revealed his glorious presence on Mt Sinai, I have now discovered is also the work of a colonial-oriented narrator who reveals the latent colonial character of YHWH, the new God of Israel.

As my analysis in this volume reveals, the narrator of Exodus portrays the God of Israel, who reveals a name, role and character to Moses, as a colonial God who not only chooses Israel as a personal people from all the people of the world, but also promises that the Israelites will be able to colonise the land of Canaan when YHWH sends terror into the Land and blots out the innocent indigenous peoples of Canaan with whom Abraham worshipped *El*, the Creator Spirit of Canaan.

YHWH, the colonial God of the old covenant of Moses, is radically different from the compassionate new covenant God of Jesus.

How can I possibly believe in the God YHWH when I have come to know, not only the God of Jesus but also the life-giving Creator Spirit of First Nations Australia?

After years of interpreting the Hebrew Scriptures and writing a range of relevant volumes, I have finally discovered that the God YHWH, who is the dominant God in most of the books in the Hebrew Scriptures, is a colonial-oriented God, a jealous God with little empathy and an Overlord ready to terrorise innocent peoples to enable YHWH's own people to establish a colony.

At 90, I am ready to dismiss the YHWH of Moses, even if that is considered the ultimate heresy. I now feel free from the colonial curse embedded in the Old Covenant, free to recognise the compassion of Christ embedded in the Christian Scriptures, and free to celebrate the relevance of the Creator Spirit experienced by Abraham and First Nations Australia.

The colonial God YHWH is, for me, outdated.

Bibliography

Albright, William, *Yahweh and the Gods of Canaan: A Historical Analysis of Two Contrasting Faiths* (New York, Doubleday Anchor, 1968).

Crotty, Robert, *Yahweh, the God of Israel* (Adelaide: Salisbury College of Advanced Education: Occasional Papers 14, 1976).

Norman Habel, *An Inconvenient Truth: Is a Green Reading of the Bible Possible?* (Adelaide: ATF Press 2009).

Habel, Norman, *Reconciliation: Searching for Australia's Soul* (Melbourne: Harper Collins, 1999).

Habel, Norman, *Acknowledgement of the Land and Faith of Aboriginal Custodians after Following the Abraham Trail* (Melbourne: Morning Star, 2018).

Harris, John, *One Blood. 2000 Years of Aboriginal Encounter with Christianity. A Story of Hope* (Sutherland: Albatross, 1990).

Pattel-Gray, Anne, *Through Aboriginal Eyes—The Cry from the Wilderness* (Geneva: WCC Publications, 1991).

Pattel-Gray, Anne, editor, *Aboriginal Spirituality, Past, Present, Future* (Melbourne: Harper Collins, 1996).

Pattel-Gray, Anne, *The Great White Flood: Racism in Australia* (Atlanta: Scholars Press, 1998).

Pattel-Gray, Anne and Norman Habel, *Decolonising the Biblical* Narrative, Volume One (Adelaide: ATF Press, 2022).

Pattel-Gray, Anne and Norman Habel, *Decolonising the Biblical Narrative, Volume Two* (Adelaide: ATF Press, 2023).

Peterson, Eugene, *The Word Made Flesh: The Language of Jesus in his Stories and Prayers* (London: Hodder and Stroughton, 2008).

Pope, Marvin, *El in the Ugaritic Texts* (Leiden: Brill, 1955).

Rainbow Spirit Elders, *Rainbow Spirit Theology. Towards an Australian Aboriginal Theology* (Melbourne: Harper Collins, 1997).

Smith, Mark S, *The Early History of God: Yahweh and Other Deities in Ancient Israel* (Grand Rapids: Eerdmans, 2002).

Zimmerli, Walther, *I Am Yahweh* (Atlanta: John Knox Press, 1982).

Printed in the USA
CPSIA information can be obtained
at www.ICGtesting.com
JSHW020855241223
54126JS00003B/190